Building
on our
strengths:

Improving education in
Aotearoa New Zealand

Building on our strengths:

Improving education in Aotearoa New Zealand

Stuart McNaughton

NZCER PRESS
Te Pakokori
Level 4, 10 Brandon St,
Wellington

www.nzcer.org.nz

© Stuart McNaughton, 2024

ISBN 978-1-99-004093-1

No part of the publication may be copied, stored, or communicated in any form by any means (paper or digital), including recording or storing in an electronic retrieval system, without the written permission of the publisher. Education institutions that hold a current licence with Copyright Licensing New Zealand may copy from this book in strict accordance with the terms of the CLNZ Licence.

A catalogue record for this book is available from the National Library of New Zealand.

Designed by Smartwork Creative

Acknowledgements

Thanks to David Choat, who asked me the provocative question, "What are we good at?", which was the catalyst for this book. Also thanks to colleagues at the Ministry of Education Te Tāhuhu o te Mātauranga, Waipapa Taumata Rau University of Auckland, and to the Forum of Chief Science Advisors, who have in their various ways reminded me how important it is to think very widely while respecting the range of evidence to make good judgements.

Most importantly, thanks to all the kaiako, teachers, whānau and families, ākonga and learners, communities, policy makers, and academics who have helped to construct, grow, critique, and value an education system with world class features. This book is dedicated to them, and to further learning from the strengths in those features, as well as from our very challenging weaknesses.

My thanks to David Ellis and Jan Eyre for their fine editorial work, and also for the clear and constructive critiques and feedback from Melinda Webber, Elaine Reese, Aaron Wilson, Trudie McNaughton, and anonymous reviewers.

Our whānau keep me honest and constantly challenge me in what we should all be better at. My thanks and aroha to them all.

About the author

Professor Stuart McNaughton ONZM is Professor of Education at Waipapa Taumata Rau University of Auckland. He has published extensively on children's development, the design of effective educational programmes for culturally and linguistically diverse populations, and cultural processes in development. He was the Founding Director of the Woolf Fisher Research Centre | Te Pūtahi, which pioneered research in design-based school change. His current research focuses on designing and testing digital tools to promote online resilience and social and cognitive skills.

He is a recipient of national and international research prizes, consults on curricula and educational interventions nationally and internationally, is a member of a number of academic bodies, and is a Senior Research Fellow at East China Normal University (Shanghai Municipal Institute for Lifelong Learning). In 2011 he was made an Officer of the New Zealand Order of Merit, and from 2014 until 2024 was Aotearoa New Zealand's inaugural Chief Education Scientific Advisor.

Contents

Acknowledgements	v
About the author	vi
Glossary	ix
Chapter 1 An introduction	**1**
Why ask the question?	1
Approaching the question (with caution)	4
Chapter 2 Being very local	**8**
Two senses of being local at the classroom level	10
Tudor England, land wars, and history	10
Mirror texts and looking outwards	13
Local control at the level of the school	15
System stewardship not control	16
Does it matter? A beginning look at the evidence	17
A COVID-19 reflection	19
What led to being local as a strength?	20
Chapter 3 Learning from only some children	**23**
The Ready to Read series	25
Beyond excellence?	27
Te Kotahitanga	28
System accommodating to some children	31
Child-centred during COVID-19?	32
Where did the strength of being child-centred come from?	35
Chapter 4 Trying to be bicultural	**38**
Native Schools: An unlikely innovation hub for te reo Māori and culturally significant practices	41
The rise of kōhanga reo, kura kaupapa Māori, and wānanga	44
Other system indicators: The curriculum, and learning te reo Māori	46
From where?	50
Chapter 5 Having partnerships	**53**
Hearing reading at home	54
Collaborative problem solving	55
Relationships and collaboration between schools	57
Collaborations between research and policy	59
Why?	61
Chapter 6 Creativity and innovation	**64**
Having a go	64
Digital Learning Objects in classrooms	66

School level creativity: Pockets of promise	67
National creativity: The School Journals	69
National creativity: A bigger picture	70
Reflections post COVID-19	71
Why?	74
Chapter 7 Not being good enough	**75**
Not good enough for equity, mixed for excellence	76
Learning from children	76
Being local	80
Trying to be bicultural	84
Relationships and collaboration	87
Being creative	90
Four big challenges to being better	92
So how do we change?	96
Being better through COVID	114
Final comments	115
References	**119**
Index	**131**

Glossary

ākonga	learner
hapū	sub-tribe
hui	a gathering, a meeting, a discussion
iwi	people, tribe
kaiako	teacher
kanohi ki te kanohi	face-to-face
kōhanga reo	Māori language preschool
kura kaupapa Māori	primary school operating under Māori custom using Māori as a medium of instruction
mana	prestige
Māori	Indigenous person/people of New Zealand
mātauranga Māori	Māori knowledge
ML	machine learning
NCEA	National Certificates of Educational Achievement
Pākehā	New Zealander of European ancestry
PIRLS	Progress in International Reading Literacy Study
PISA	Programme for International Student Assessment
SES	socio-economic status
tamariki	children

tāngata Tiriti	non-Māori who acknowledge and respect Te Tiriti o Waitangi
tāngata whenua	Indigenous people of Aotearoa New Zealand
tauiwi	non-Maori people of Aotearoa New Zealand
te ao Māori	the Māori world, including Māori worldview
TIMMS	Trends in International Mathematics and Science Study
tuakana-teina	older or more expert peers guiding younger, less expert peers
wānanga	tertiary institution catering for Māori learning needs
whānau	family, including extended family
whanaungatanga	relationships

Chapter 1

An introduction

Why ask the question?

The education system in Aotearoa New Zealand faces longstanding and seemingly intractable challenges. The list includes our equity profile, revealed over decades of national and international progress and achievement data. It also includes the overall quality of the system, again judged by national and international benchmarking of progress and achievement. While the OECD, through its Programme for International Student Assessment (PISA), identifies Aotearoa New Zealand as overall a high-quality system but with low equity, there are compelling areas where the quality is not as good as it should be. These include the slower than expected progress and low achievement in literacy and numeracy between Years 4 and 8. Those years are also years where the gaps between children from Māori and Pasifika communities and from communities with fewer material resources become even more obvious (for a recent summary, see Ministry of Education, 2023a).

Importantly, the national and international databases are not limited to curriculum learning areas such as literacy, mathematics, and science. They also include measures of valued outcomes that reflect the wellbeing of students. In these areas, we are also wanting relative to other countries, with high rates of not feeling one belongs at school, high rates of bullying, and high rates of disengagement (Ministry of Education, 2020a). The picture for students with disabilities, including those who are neurodivergent, has been described as "devastating" (Hood & Hume, 2024).

Solving these challenges at a system level has proven difficult, despite the long-term commitment and effort of educators, policy makers, researchers, and communities. At the time of writing there are many system initiatives. There is a wide-ranging curriculum "refresh" in process, changes to the senior secondary examinations system are occurring, and a new way of funding schools to overcome barriers caused by conditions of material hardship has been put in place. There are also redesigns of teaching and learning in early learning settings and schools, such as scaling up a programme to increase levels of self-regulation, and intensive school-by-school changes to increase engagement of ākonga Māori. There are schools developing innovative digital pedagogies and taking these to a near national scale.

This book does not review the evidence supporting these shifts, nor their impacts. It starts from a different point. The claim of this book is that Aotearoa New Zealand needs to preserve and build on the strengths we have to achieve our goals for excellence and equity. The catalyst for this was a question posed late in 2019 by a political advisor to the then Minister of Education. We had been discussing recent developments in educational policy, including those in other countries. We had revisited the lessons from Finland, the sometime poster child of the OECD international comparisons. Faced with another book about how good Finland is, he asked: "So tell me, what are we good at?"

That is such a good question, for three reasons. Firstly, to change a system for the better one needs to know more than what the weaknesses are. We should know what the points of strength are, so that these can be built on or used as leverage, or at least not compromised in any further changes. A fundamental principle in learning is to start where the learner is "at" (Puzio et al., 2020). This turns out to be a principle generalisable to less granular levels, such as enabling groups of schools or even district-level systems to solve challenges to being more effective, as our bourgeoning improvement science shows (Bryk et al., 2015). Context strengths need to be known to scale up new ways of working, and this is not just a peculiarity of education (Shelton et al., 2018). There is also the evidence from interventions and curriculum focus in schools that can show a positive change in a target area of learning, only to also find a negative impact on an area that was a strength previously (Engel et al., 2016; Borman et al., 2008).

Secondly, it is a good question because of a form of meta-awareness at a system level. If the lessons from Finland are anything to go by, knowing what we are good at means we are better able to reflect on the system's attributes, possibly using them as a test for how fit for purpose new developments are. This evidence-informed awareness provides the capability for continuous improvement.

There is a third reason it is a good question. I have become increasingly uncomfortable with the concentration only on what we don't do well, the persistent pessimism in many academic and policy debates. I want to add to that with a focus on "what works for whom, under what conditions and at scale" (Bryk, et al., 2015, p. 13): the question of what it is possible to improve on, and how we can do that. Ultimately, this means answers can be experimental in nature. What if we did more of X, or made X more consistent, or added value to X (and let's test it out)?

This question of our strengths came very early in my role as the Chief Education Scientific Advisor to the Ministry of Education. One Minister with whom I worked said, "I'm sick of hearing about all the problems. Tell me the 10 things we need to do." I returned the next day with a briefing paper containing a short list of five. These partly form the basis for this book, and I return to that list in the final chapter.

The Minister's question was an appropriate provocation. We are well aware of the problems. We know we have systemic bias and racism. We know our ākonga do not do very well in science and mathematics, and this is related to matters of capacity, qualification, and specialisation in primary schools. Disengagement from school is palpable. How many more times do we resort to platitudes about the "quality" of early childhood provisions when successive Governments ask for proof, for evidence of "effectiveness" or added value, when we have known for a long time our children arrive at school already suffering from pervasive differences in educational capital?

Approaching the question (with caution)

My approach to the question "What do we do well?" has been to look at the evidence, in two ways. One is to demonstrate that the identified strength is actually a feature of our system, and the second is to show that the strength can be associated with being successful. There are obvious areas of success to celebrate, even in the national and international monitoring. Overall, as I have noted, the OECD rates our system as high quality and, despite worrying downward trajectories in some areas developing around 2009, some of the international assessments still show us to be with high-banded countries in reading and literacy. But this success hides our poor equity profile. Relative to other countries with whom we benchmark, our 15-year-olds are more advanced than many in media and information literacy.[1] Their collaborative problem solving on computers (May, 2017) in a game-based format is also a relative strength. Yet another example is the minimal effect, if any, on reading achievement of successive lockdowns during COVID-19, shown in both the national databases and the international comparisons (Ministry of Education, 2021a; Ministry of Education, 2023b). But each of these examples, and others reviewed in this book, come with the qualification that alongside this success is our dire equity profile. They are limited successes.

I will return to these and other examples, drawing on my discipline knowledge as a developmental and educational psychologist, my experiences as a researcher with schools and communities, and more recently being in a national policy advisory role.

To justify the claims of a strength, I also draw on the historical record. I am not an historian by training nor a political analyst. Nor am I a Māori scholar or an expert on Māori education. These are major caveats for what follows because it contains matters of historical record, and there are comments on Māori education, which I have tried to present with humility, care, and accuracy.

The limitations revealed by the evidence come in several forms. In some cases, they are to do with too much variability. What we do well

---

1   https://www.educationcounts.govt.nz/publications/series/PISA/pisa-2018

waxes and wanes depending on policies and practices in the system. In other cases, the strength is limited in terms of coverage; it is not as present everywhere in the system as it should be. Most importantly, there is the limitation revealed when the criterion is: "Has it been sufficient to solve inequalities in the system?". Specifically, is it sufficient to solve the unequal outcomes in educational success for Māori and Pasifika children and for children from stressed material conditions of inadequate housing, low income, and low employment?

The answer to that question is obvious. In short, a resounding no. It has been an overall unequal system since inception as a colonial enterprise, although with pockets where the trend has been bucked. These pockets were present very early, even in the so-called Native Schools, and they are present in impressive examples in local pockets where an educationally significant difference has been made (Simon & Smith, 2001; Jesson et al., 2018). The argument here is that if we built on these strengths, making them more pervasive, better implemented, even stronger, the inequities might be able to be solved at a system level.

Solving our problems, particularly those to do with equity, cannot be achieved by the education system alone. The weight of evidence is that the system is limited to the degree that the society at large is inequitable. Without reductions in poverty and the multifactorial disadvantages which are getting greater, it is a Herculean task for education alone. The instances in schools where it has been done literally come at great cost. It takes considerable resourcing of time, energy, and funding.

In each of the five chapters on our strengths I keep the high quality with low equity designation in mind when identifying what a strength might be and how we could be better with that strength. In each of the five strengths, I provide evidence at multiple levels. These levels are the individual teacher, schools, and the wider system, in order to show this is a relatively generalised strength. Relatively, because in each area of strength the evidence clearly is there is still more that we could do and there is the ever-present threat of too much variability. This is what the last chapter deals with. What should we be better at doing, given these strengths?

In each of the chapters the argument is that we need to preserve and build on the strengths, as judged against both excellence and equity criteria. There is an introduction to the evidence to support the claim that these are strengths in terms of valued educational outcomes judged against both excellence and equity criteria. More evidence is introduced in the final chapter, which proposes specific structural, pedagogical, and other system changes that might now take place to build on this strength.

The five strengths are these:

1. **Being local.** Our educational system assumes and requires a great deal of local expertise. Being local can be seen at all levels: the individual teacher with a class of learners and their whānau; the school and its relationships with communities; groups of schools; and the roles and responsibilities of the national agency.

2. **Learning from *some* children.** We have a history of putting children's experiences and identity at the centre of classroom teaching and learning. By privileging children in this way, we have also attempted to learn from them.

3. ***Trying* to be bicultural.** This chapter makes a distinction between our progress and what is still left to achieve, despite what the system has been trying to do for decades. It is also meant to acknowledge a struggle by Māori for cultural identity in a schooling system largely created by non-Māori.

4. **Having partnerships.** Partnerships of all types are ubiquitous in our educational system. As with the other strengths, this strength can be seen at various levels of the system, the first at the beginning of children's formal schooling with families and whānau. Partnerships can be found at all levels of our system including between policymakers and researchers, through which local research has informed policy and where there have been long periods of collaboration.

5. **Creation and innovation.** We support local innovation and creativity. This can be seen in Māori educational designs and in non-Māori education, again at all levels. Innovation and

creativity have been valued in pre- and post-colonial times and we value creativity in teaching and schools.

Addendum: a pandemic. I started writing this book before our experience with the COVID-19 pandemic. Each of the five strengths, and our weaknesses, were on display during the phases of the national response to the pandemic. The pandemic exposed areas of inadequacy, but it also highlighted the strengths. Each chapter provides a brief summary of what we learned about both.

Chapter 2

Being very local

If, as a beginning teacher in Aotearoa New Zealand, you wanted a fully scripted account, moment by moment, of what you should do from arriving at school through the pedagogical and content-laden day and beyond, you would be out of luck. The unrefreshed Aotearoa New Zealand curriculum document (English medium) currently is a brief 49 pages (Ministry of Education, 2007), hardly a "how to do it" manual. Seven of those pages explain the iconography, and are foreword and contents pages. Few pages are devoted to the learning areas. Mathematics and Statistics, for example, has four, one of which is a full-page photo of a learner.

This is not all there is to draw on, of course. There is the training and then immersion in practice that one receives as a teacher. There are resources on websites which provide progressions and exemplars in the learning areas such as Mathematics and Statistics, and Science, and there have been years of professional development and learning. But the brevity of the curriculum statements illustrates one basic property of our system—it assumes and requires a great deal of local expertise. We are of course engaged in a curriculum refresh process which will provide more detail. But the resultant documents, if the one that is first off the block is anything to go by, retain that expectation of and respect for teachers. Thank goodness.

Being local can be seen at all levels: the individual teacher with a class of learners and their whānau; the school and its relationships with its communities; within groups of schools; and the roles and responsibilities of the national agency.

This is not accidental, or a by-product of something else, such as keeping costs for publishing the curriculum down. The deliberate and explicit expectation is to be local, captured in what one Minister of Education popularised as the "local curriculum".

One teacher I know exemplifies what a local curriculum looks like, at least at the micro level of explaining a concept. He was concerned that successive Year 9 students entering the secondary school where he was Head of Department for mathematics did not have sufficient understanding of the concept of negative number.

His solution? Here is a confession of sorts. He and I follow the local rugby league team, the only local team in the Australian National Rugby League competition. One disastrous year (I have to say among all too many), the New Zealand Warriors exceeded their salary cap. The salary cap is a device to reduce the likelihood that richer clubs get an edge on others simply by spending up large on marquee players, and outbidding poorer clubs.

The New Zealand Warriors were docked 4 points for this misdemeanour. They started the year 4 points in arrears. The teacher capitalised on this well-known local disaster. He asked his Year 9 class, full of Māori and Pasifika students who followed or knew about the New Zealand Warriors, how many points they would have if they won the first game. Winning would give them 2 points. Without hesitation came the reply, "Minus 2, Sir." How many points would they have if they won the next game? "Zero points, Sir." Those Year 9s got the concept of negative number pretty quickly.

This sounds like an obvious and simple pedagogical move: contextualise the concept. It is widely expected that this is what teachers can and should do, exemplified by the 49-page curriculum. But it also now very obvious that this is a difficult ask. I was once asked by a Minister of Education, "Why can't teachers do it?". The answer is that it is very difficult to do effectively. You need to have expertise for not only determining what your students' local knowledge and experiences might be, but also how their knowledge might represent the deep conceptual principles of the curriculum domain. And then, you need the expertise to draw students' attention to the deep principle from the familiar knowledge.

Despite the big ask, it turns out we are very good at capitalising on being local. We have to be. At each of the levels there is evidence that what we have done, and what we do, can be highly effective. From a variety of angles this is a strength. What follows are some examples of that strength at each level of the system, and an introduction to the evidence that this strength can contribute to an even better system.

Two senses of being local at the classroom level

This strength has some perverse features. The strength at the classroom level looks different in different areas of the curriculum. One such feature was on display when I went to school. There was no local history to speak of, at least not in my classrooms. This was in contrast to reading comprehension in the English curriculum, which had a core set of texts for the middle primary years delivered by the then School Publications Branch of the Department of Education. The texts were known as the New Zealand School Journals, which did feature local context.[2]

Tudor England, land wars, and history

Up to the early 2000s, Tudor and Stuart England, Black Civil Rights, and Vietnam were more popular choices for teaching history than the sometimes disturbing pre- and postcolonial history of Aotearoa New Zealand (Davison, 2021). The reach of the colonising country and the academic study of history meant history had an Anglophile, or at least offshore, lens.

---

2   See *A nest of singing birds: 100 years of the New Zealand School Journal* by Gregory O'Brien published by Learning Media for the centenary of the School Journal in 2007.

We had academics whose field at university was Tudor England who taught many of the teachers. The loose history specifications in the curriculum enabled these interests to predominate, which in one sense paradoxically illustrates the theme about local decision-making about content. They could take their preparation and turn the loose specifications in the curriculum document into a curriculum at the local level of one's classroom.

The history of being able to pass exams by answering questions about Tudor England in our senior secondary exams might illustrate that our teachers were very capable of figuring out how to design the local curriculum for Tudor history, without that detailed specification. But being able to do this is different from the lack of local history in the sense of our own histories. This is a very different test of being able to make this area of the curriculum local.

Partly in response to this, in 1998 one of New Zealand's most locally enthused historians, James Belich, produced a powerful five-part documentary on the New Zealand Wars which argued that the existing accounts had got the seemingly simple question of who won the four distinct wars wrong (Belich, 1998). He also demonstrated, counter to received wisdom, that Māori showed enormous tactical and military skill, claiming that they invented trench warfare long before the First World War.

In part, the series and the book upon which it was based was Belich's response to what he saw as the pre-eminence of other histories, such as Tudor England, in history teaching. He had joined an earlier non-Māori historian, Professor Sir Keith Sinclair, and a growing number of Māori historians to "get kids to look at the history outside of their window."

Perhaps Belich worried too much. In pockets there have always been teachers who have used local history, such as the history of the land wars, to design the local curriculum despite the Tudors—as accounts about teaching in the Native Schools suggest. The most recent examples of local curriculum at work are leveraging off new technologies. One is a game designed by Ruth Lemon at the University of Auckland.[3] She was moved to create the game, originally in the form of the well-known game Trivial Pursuit, because her first-year Bachelor of Education students struggled with the version of history they'd been taught at school. It was a means of engaging them in the history of relationships between Māori and Pākehā in the years before the Treaty was signed. Hohi, which is the name of the game, was the first European settlement and the site of the first European-style school, which opened in 1816.

So the curriculum requires teachers to be curriculum design experts in their own classroom in their own localities. That is the first sense of being local. But a more fundamental expression occurs when they draw on what is actually local. Unfortunately, not every history teacher has localised the study of our history, and as submissions in 2019 to the Education and Workforce Select Committee pointedly noted, it has not been mandatory (Manning & Cooper, 2018). There wasn't a prescribed syllabus.

Arguably, given the expected design expertise, there shouldn't be prescription, just a willingness to use the local context to illustrate the deep and generalisable principles of historical research. But the variability has meant that decisions to refresh the curriculum have recognised the need to address the Achilles' heel in this strength—the perennial problem of variable or inconsistent quality in being local.

When I initially drafted this last section, before the COVID-19 event, the then Government had acted to make the teaching of Aotearoa New Zealand histories mandatory. In 2021, a draft of the curriculum content for Aotearoa New Zealand's histories was made available for public feedback. Following the consultation and reworking, from 2023 Aotearoa New Zealand's histories has been taught in all schools and kura. There is a section in the final chapter that references where the original consultation landed because it illustrates so well this commitment to acknowledging local history.

This is a profound move. In a way it is a recognition of the strength of being (and the need to be) local. But the vision is also to do with

---

3   https://cybersoul.co.nz/hohi1816.html

citizenship: knowing what our shared history is, and being able to understand and appreciate what we have and haven't achieved as a country and what we need to achieve.

However, I know from what I have outlined above that to do this well every teacher of history—which also means *all* primary school teachers, as well as the generalist social studies teachers and the specialist history teachers—need the requisite skills and knowledge to design appropriately. If they can't, it will be like what I experienced as a doctoral student at the University of Kansas. Every student had to take a semester course in Western Civilisation, philosophy from Plato to Bertrand Russell (that dates me!). "Western Civ", as it was affectionately known, was universally hated by students. It had a compliance cost and was perceived as a barrier. It was an imposition. We mustn't let this sense of imposition and irrelevance happen, as illustrated by the framework and required content in Aotearoa New Zealand's histories which set the requirements for what students need to "understand, know and do" at all levels.[4]

Mirror texts and looking outwards

There is a counter story to the one of NZ history teaching. It is the use of vernacular and local images and stories as the basis of the nationally used texts for learning to read in the early years (Education Gazette, 2014). Where historians in Aotearoa New Zealand had not embedded NZ history into business as usual, literacy teachers had achieved a national presence for local content and an international reputation for innovation and excellence.

More of this unique resource is described in the next chapter. But the history and evidence of effectiveness of these books is the reason why many historians are passionate about local histories, and why a core set of national expectations for teaching local history was needed.

The reason is captured in a metaphor about texts which is used by my colleague Aaron Wilson. He is a scholar of English and adolescent literacy and for him the metaphor is about narrative fiction

---

4 https://aotearoahistories.education.govt.nz/about/content-structure

texts, which can be simply categorised into two sorts, in terms of their *relationship to the reader.* There are mirror texts or there are window texts.[5] Admittedly there are now also hybrid texts, if you like, with split screens and even one-way screens, to stretch the metaphor.

Mirror texts reflect the reader's background, lived experience and more broadly identity. The window texts are those that look out into the unfamiliar, out into a world beyond one's own immediate and familiar one. The former, mirror texts, have a general property long recognised in the science of reading. The closer the match between the text content and the reader's background knowledge the greater the comprehension, and we now know its importance for identity formation and feeling one's background is respected in schools (Hattan et al., 2023; Lee, 2007). We better engage with a book and understand it better if we are able to see ourselves, our identity, our knowledge, our place, and our language in that text.

We have known for more than 40 years that this background knowledge matters to comprehension. Assuming the basic skills in getting words off the page (decoding) are present—which most students have very early on in literacy instruction—what really determines comprehension is what you know about the content, what language (especially vocabulary) you have to engage with that content, and whether you have the capability to apply this knowledge strategically.

Students need both sorts of texts. If one is restricted to mirrors there is a risk of not being able to learn about what is new and understand what is unfamiliar, let alone not being able to generalise skills well learned with familiar contexts. But confronted only with windows, some students—at least early on in their learning—are more likely to be disengaged and struggle with comprehension.

But here is the nub of the equity problem. The texts that children tend to get after learning to read, when reading in different subject areas, more generally favour the children from certain communities. This is the challenge. Sadly, only about a quarter of our Year 4 and 8

---

5   https://scenicregional.org/wp-content/uploads/2017/08/Mirrors-Windows-and-Sliding-Glass-Doors.pdf

students reported in a national survey in 2014 they had the opportunity to read books that reflect their social and cultural identities. We are good at providing mirror texts,[6] but need to be better.

Local control at the level of the school

The most obvious expression of being local at a system level is the autonomy of schools. A relatively extreme form of self-management introduced in 1989 made each school self-managing (Robinson et al., 2011). Each school is governed by its own board of parent-elected representatives who, among other responsibilities, appoint and appraise the school's principal. The board, which includes the school principal, has discretion to govern the school as it sees fit, subject to the existing law (Education Act 1989, s. 6). School boards must report to the Ministry of Education and to their communities about student achievement and are reviewed approximately every 3 years by the national Education Review Office.

The board is required by legislation to govern the school. It sets the local expressions of policy; ensures the educational objectives are upheld; and it appoints, suspends, or dismisses school staff including the principal. The board's role is so encompassing that it has left the Ministry of Education with limited powers to intervene in schools about which they might have concerns.

This is a form of local democratic control. The board members are elected and they represent the community of the school. In reality there are some serious unintended consequences, which have become so pressing that there have been moves to recover more collective units comprised of numbers of schools acting together to promote valued educational outcomes, possibly even with shared governance.

But the idea of decision making devolved to the level of a school or a collective of schools reflects the strong thread of localisation. It also reflects a system-level view which is strongly held.

---

6   https://nmssa-production.s3.amazonaws.com/documents/Reading_SOF.pdf

System stewardship not control

A previous Secretary of Education, Peter Hughes, made the role of the Ministry of Education as a government agency very clear: it is one of stewardship. After his time as Secretary he became State Services Commissioner, the head of the Public Service in Aotearoa New Zealand. In 2017 his updated description of the role of the State Services, which includes the Ministry of Education, was entitled *Free and Frank Advice and Policy Stewardship*.[7] This framework continues to set the stewardship role across Crown agencies.

This view has been implicit in the national education system for many years. Peter Hughes made it explicit and clarified what it meant. There is relatively limited central control over many aspects of the compulsory school sector.

One example is how a major educational goal, to promote the wellbeing of students, is implemented at a system level. Firstly, and to reiterate the point about local curricula, there is loose specification in *The New Zealand Curriculum* (Ministry of Education, 2007) around how schools might promote a set of competencies associated with wellbeing that are key to learning in each curriculum area. These "key competencies" are identified and include aspects of wellbeing such as *managing self*, *relating to others*, and *participating and contributing*.

Consistent with the aspirational and broad nature of *The New Zealand Curriculum*, and the idea of local control, there are no mandates or specific prescriptions for how the skills relating to wellbeing might be developed. There are no agreed and required measures of the development of these skills in the schooling sector. Indeed, it is expected there will be variation in how promotion might be done. The document notes:

> Schools need to consider how each of these aspects of the curriculum will be promoted and developed in teaching and learning. They can do this in different ways. (Ministry of Education, 2007, p. 37)

---

7   https://www.publicservice.govt.nz/guidance/guide-he-aratohu/guidance/free-and-frank-advice-and-policy-stewardship/

In addition to the curriculum framework for promoting wellbeing, there are national regulations that mandate school responsibilities. These require the local managing body, the Board of Trustees elected from the local community, to create safe and secure environments. There are codes of conduct for teachers that include their role in promoting wellbeing. The major mechanisms identified for meeting these mandatory requirements are through school values being made explicit and embedded in everyday practices where students feel valued, included, supported, and safe. But the overriding point is that the system expects the "what and how" of wellbeing promotion to be the responsibility of those in the local context.

Does it matter? A beginning look at the evidence

So we have a strength at being local, but does it matter? Answering this of course depends on what you value. Answered more fully in the final chapter, the question is whether it matters to the equity and excellence challenges outlined in the introduction. Here is a first look at this question.

Some positive but essentially correlational evidence comes from our design of early literacy instruction, which had roots in local innovations and capitalises on local implementations. The previously described use of the mirror texts for beginning reading was quintessentially a local project supporting the teaching of foundational reading and writing.

The first of the international comparisons of literacy achievement, conducted by the International Association for the Evaluation of Educational Achievement (IEA) in 1992, provided one indicator of effectiveness of instruction in the early years (Elley, 1992). It showed that after 5 years of schooling, our 10-year-olds' reading comprehension was among the highest in the world. The locally designed books for learning to read, together with a meaning-focused comprehensive form of foundational learning, had been in place nationally for 30 years (McNaughton, 2022). It has remained very high in international terms, with a significant decrease notable from 2011 (Chamberlain, 2019). The first indication we had of how well we stack up in an international sense in literacy instruction suggested that being local was associated with excellence.

There are other components of our beginning literacy programme established in the 1960s, some which have sound experimental evidence. A practice we will describe in greater detail in the chapter on collaboration is engaging families in children's early reading (Alton-Lee, 2003). Sending books home for families and whānau members to hear beginning readers read was an early innovation, unique in international terms. This innovation, begun in local contexts before the 1960s, became nationally embedded following a major statement on early instruction, notably entitled, given the loose designation, "*Suggestions* for teaching reading in Infant classes" (my emphasis) (Simpson, 1962).

Overall, we may have cause to celebrate this early and continuing metric about quality of our literacy instruction. But this high quality is tarnished by the equity data. Inequalities are consistently present across gender, ethnicity, and socioeconomic status (SES) groups. The case of mathematics further illustrates the conundrum—being high quality but low on equity outcomes. The renowned statistical scientist David Spiegelhalter claimed in a recent book that Aotearoa New Zealand leads the world in statistics education (Speigelhalter, 2019). His claim is based on curriculum materials in statistics that foreground local problem-solving cycles.

There is evidence, including document analysis of many senior assessment items, which supports the conclusion that this is bread and butter to statistics teachers. Spiegelhalter therefore is right in terms of the curriculum, and probably right at the level of individual maths teachers at secondary school where statistics is a specialist subject. Not surprisingly, we are nationally relatively better at statistics than we are at other areas of mathematics (Ministry of Education, 2020b).

But in the primary years it certainly is not the case of high-quality maths achievement. Our national monitoring suggests very low rates of progress in mathematics from Year 4 to Year 8.[8] And the effectiveness is not widespread enough, or consistent enough, or perhaps localised enough, to solve the inequalities that also exist in mathematics achievement. Once again, we could do better.

What about the governance of schools at a local level? There have been positive impacts of the increased "ownership" of schools at the local community level. But the weaknesses, which were not predicted in the original design, have become very obvious; for example, increasing competitiveness between schools and increasing ethnic and socio-economic status polarisation of school mix.[9] In addition, it has at best restricted the degree to which effective practices have been able to be identified, tested, and shared across schools, let alone taken to scale nationally.

Structural changes have been made and other major ones are in the wind. Communities of Learning | Kāhui Ako (local aggregations of 5–10 schools both primary and secondary) have been, in a very Aotearoa New Zealand way, *encouraged* to develop. New positions have been created and funded for within-school and between-school leaders, specifically to identify and build more effective practices at the local level.

As I write this there is ongoing deliberation over details of further structural changes. Redesigning could include hubs at a local level which pool teaching and learning resources, including those for specialist learning needs, and manage and resource those aspects of schools' functions which take the focus away from learning as business as usual (such as finances).

A COVID-19 reflection

An interesting test of whether "being local" is a strength was created by the pandemic. This really invites a series of questions ranging from whether it was possible to be local in the sense I have described, through to what would now count as being local in online teaching

---

8   https://nmssa-production.s3.amazonaws.com/documents/2018_NMSSA_MATHEMATICS_SUM.pdf

9   https://conversation.education.govt.nz/conversations/tomorrows-schools-review/

and learning. There is little systematic evidence to draw on to answer these questions.

However, what is obvious is that teachers felt the stress of not having in real time some of the markers—the bits of formal and informal evidence—that they use to judge their effectiveness and to decide about next steps. Despite this, a quick search of online resources developed by teachers indicates considerable use of local events, shared knowledge with students, and the local conditions created by the lockdown in their resources.

At a system level the agile response meant a number of generic and local resources needed to be developed by teachers. The advice to teachers and even the generic resources still had the features of drawing on what had been local and urging teachers to use their knowledge of their students and their communities. Many online resources were developed by teachers rather than being taken "off the shelf", more so probably with teachers who were part of well-experienced digital schools and clusters of schools.

What led to being local as a strength?

The patterns at classroom, school, and national levels suggest a recurring theme of being local. From where did this strength come? Two patterns from our histories might have played a part. We can see it in the precolonial patterns recorded in oral histories of the nature of teaching and learning. We can see the localising of pedagogy and curriculum also at the very beginnings of colonial schooling.

An embedded or apprenticeship style of teaching and learning was present in precolonial times. It is still present. Pakariki (Paki) Harrison was the master carver for Tāne-nui-ā-Rangi, the marae at Waipapa Taumata Rau University of Auckland, which opened in 1988 (Walker, 2008). It is a superb, deeply spiritual centre defining the heart of the university. Like all marae, it is a place for the tāngata whenua to stand with mana. Paki was a contemporary carver. But his learning reflects abiding patterns that others have argued predate formal schooling brought by the colonists.

As Paki told it, he learned through a combination of being in the local site and observing and engaging in real acts as a child, playing alongside the carvers taking up the local challenge to carve the house. But this deliberate play was combined with equally deliberate guidance provided by the carvers and later in more formal settings.

Paki's story could also be used to illuminate the strength discussed in the next chapter—being learner-centred. But here it is an instance of the idea of a local curriculum reflecting ancient ways and providing a legacy for us today.

The second historical foundation could be in colonial schooling itself. Despite the colonial enterprise which had a "civilising" agenda, some of the so-called Native Schools were sites of innovation (Simon & Smith, 2001). In keeping with a closely related strength about adaptiveness and creativity (see Chapter 6), some teachers who taught in these schools also built on and innovated with local resources. Some deliberately rejected the inspectors' directions and designed their own local resources, including the use of te reo Māori at a time when it was outlawed.

This of course begs the question of why some teachers did not toe the colonial line, while others did. Why did some, like Sylvia Ashton-Warner and others, resist and invent alternatives to the required texts featuring English scenes and English meanings, rejecting these as very opaque window texts and creating mirror books instead?

Judith Simon and Linda Tuhiwai Smith (2001) estimate that about 20% of the Native Schools teachers joined as "idealistic entrants", as distinct from "pragmatic entrants". They were primarily interested in living and working amongst Māori and were concerned with their interest. The innovating teachers had deliberately chosen to teach in Native Schools, sometimes responding to promotional incentives, but also to lifestyle values. New and exciting theories of the human mind also played a part, all of which contributed to attributes that drove innovation from local sites.

In Sylvia Ashton-Warner's case, for example, her mother was a teacher. She married a teacher. At her suggestion, after teaching at small rural schools, the couple moved to the first of several Native Schools. In addition to this commitment and deliberate desire to engage with tāngata whenua, she developed a theory of motivated or organic learning drawing on psychoanalytic theory. This came early in her career when she was treated by a neurologist who it appears mentored her in psychoanalytic theory and with her writing (Jones & Middleton, 2009). Thankfully this sense of working things out on the ground seems to have become part of the DNA of our teachers and our system as a whole.

Chapter 3

Learning from only some children

My background as a developmental psychologist leads me to think of educational systems as providing a secondary socialisation. We design schools to socialise children into sets of norms and values, and to support them to become knowledgeable with the skills and practices that a society and educational system value. The psychological process involves a dance between educational structures and developmental systems. A child learns and develops through interactions and relationships channelled by the institutional norms and practices afforded by curricula and pedagogy.

There is both overlap and idiosyncrasy across national public systems in how they manage this socialisation process. Take the case of wellbeing. Educational authorities across many countries have explicit aims to promote the social, emotional, and personal development of their children—essentially their wellbeing.[10] At the most generic level what is meant by wellbeing may be similar across countries, such as the group of attributes, skills, and emotions that enable one to flourish in life.

But systems also differ in detail. For example, traditional Chinese education has emphasised values of respect, honesty, kindness, and strong human bonding based on the concept of *ren*: that is, being

---

10   See discussion and references in McNaughton & Li (2018).

humane especially in relationship to others, which is somewhat different from the primarily individual-centric focus in OECD measures of wellbeing. The Chinese concept resonates with those enshrined in the curriculum of Aotearoa New Zealand, but there are also distinct emphases and framing in our system. These include respect, for oneself and for others and their human rights. Personal attributes such as integrity, perseverance, and curiosity are identified, but alongside the valuing of diversity and equity. The values reflect our indigenous concepts, such as those of whanaungatanga (relationship).

The core societal narratives around socialisation provide an orientation to children. What may also differ across countries is how societies position children, and, in particular, in what ways they are "child-centred". For a large part of the 20th century there were efforts to move from passively following prescribed steps to the child being more of an active agent—engaging, innovating, and playing with complex thoughts and skills. New Zealand educators in the 1930s and 40s, including Clarence Beeby, the Secretary of Education, were influential in the local version of the movement to being child-centred (McDonald, 2002).

Unfortunately, this idea of being child-centred is one of many concepts in education which can be difficult to pin down. A closer look shows that despite the policy narrative, there is many a slip twixt cup (policy) and lip (reality), as the Canadian psychologist David Olson observed in his 2003 book on psychological theory and educational reform (Olson, 2003). He argued that despite repeated attempts at reform, schools that claimed to be child-centred in the United States were anything but that. His reason? Despite curricula and pedagogical theory designed to promote independence and child agency, the institutional structures still delivered highly structured and relatively passive forms of learning.

This rather bleak picture does not apply to Aotearoa New Zealand. We have a history of putting children's experiences and identity at the centre of classroom teaching and learning, and arguably have had more success with it. By privileging children in this way, we have also attempted to learn from them. But as with being local, we could do better. That is why the title of this chapter is qualified by the adjectival phrase "only some". There is more to do to use the strength of learning from all children to meet both goals of excellence and equity. But the introduction to the evidence for its significance suggests we really should do more.

The Ready to Read series

The first piece of evidence for the generalised presence is about a series more compelling to me and longer lasting than any on Netflix. In 1940 Sylvia Ashton-Warner was teaching in a Native (i.e., Māori) School at Pipiriki, on the Whanganui River. Later she moved to a remote rural Māori school on the East Coast of the North Island. At both these schools she faced a problem of her own making. She found that what she was prepared and expected to do in teaching her children to read in English was inappropriate. She was meant to use the departmental books set in the English countryside, with nightingales and snow-covered hills, and have tamariki (children) learning to read from the antics of children quintessentially of the British Isles—Janet and John.

She began designing books for children to learn to read which drew on their everyday experiences and their everyday language. They were in her words "organic". Simplified structure and vocabulary notwithstanding, she used events and words which were locally familiar and imbued with meaning, such as "haka dance", "ghost", and "kiss". Many of these words would be deemed low frequency in our lexicon, especially for young school children, and certainly not easily "decodable".

Of crucial importance to my argument is that it turns out that this wasn't an isolated case of being child-centred. Sylvia Ashton-Warner was not the only teacher in a Native School doing this (Simon & Smith, 2001). A number of teachers reached the same conclusion and designed child-centred books. This was something akin to the evolutionary process described by Stephen Jay Gould of convergent evolution: spontaneous and parallel forms of adaptation breaking out across species (Gould, 1989). But unlike an evolutionary process, this was very active and intentional. It was a form of resistance to the colonial enterprise and a testament to the power of our innovation, albeit in pockets.

Recognising what we are good at, such as learning from children, also uncovers an entrenched challenge in our system. It is turning the pockets into a full garment. The problem of taking innovation to scale across a system turns out to be very, very difficult. Thankfully, the case of the organic readers is the counterpoint because in time these became the core resources across our entire system—not without challenge, it must be said.

This deliberate use of children's own experiences and language as a basis for early learning had widespread significance. In time it came to be business as usual, expressed in the core national reading series. This is one of the few examples of where we were able to take an innovation to scale nationally with remarkable consequences. It happened in a very Kiwi way.

In 1959 Myrtle Simpson was appointed by the then Department of Education to be editor of a new local series of "infant" readers to replace the Janet and John series, which over years had been systematically undermined by teachers such as Sylvia Ashton-Warner and found to be wanting. Through what would now be called focus group methods and co-design, draft books were developed with the teachers who had been busily innovating in Native Schools. In 1963 the first batch of 12 storybooks and six readers containing several stories was released alongside a handbook for teachers.

The title of the handbook is very revealing, as I have noted already. It recognised the first of the strengths of the system—the agency of teachers. Its title was *Suggestions for Teaching Reading in Infant Classes*—suggestions, not prescriptions. A fundamental message in the handbook was that teaching reading was "most effectively done in the course of a flexible programme, which gives the teacher the opportunity to observe the children at work". The books and the pedagogy entailed were nationally implemented, and for 40 years were the basis upon which we became a world leader in early literacy instruction, evidenced by the first of the international comparisons of reading achievement in primary schools noted earlier.

The building blocks for this nationally scaled innovation included policy makers and professional experts working together, a centralised system for making and distributing the books which made core resources freely available in a non-commercialised environment, a shared understanding of what children needed, leaders to make it happen, and fewer than 6 degrees of separation between each of these agents (likely fewer than 2 degrees).

It turns out this collectiveness and closeness between participants is not just present in the education system, supporting my claim this is something we are good at. It is identified as one component for why we are so creative in our social impact advertisements. The most recent example (described more in the chapter on being creative) has been an ad designed to keep children safe from online pornography. The whole campaign, which included billboards, posters, print ads, social media, and its own website, was created over a very short period of time (4 weeks) through close co-design with the clients, who included the government agencies of Internal Affairs, the Ministry of Education, and the Police.

Beyond excellence?

This innovating based on children's worlds was not limited to reading. In 1949 Elwyn Richardson was posted to Ōruaiti School in a remote part of Northland. His background was in palaeontology. Like Ashton-Warner, he discarded the official syllabus and turned to the children's lives and immediate environment for the basis of his curriculum (MacDonald, 2016).

This grounded the teaching in the children's interests. Richardson used their lives in mustering and fishing, dealing with infestations of moths, the spread of gorse, or sanitary levels in the local swimming holes, as a basis for what came to be called the language experience approach to writing. He developed a pedagogical concept of integration which meant that creativity in dance, language, painting, and clay work could provide a seamless connection between his students' informal knowledge and the literacy skills.

We have been excellent at being attuned to children in literacy, but not, it must be repeated, equitably and universally. We have also had the unwanted moniker of being a world leader in what is variously represented as a long tail of lower achievement or a stretched distribution—the OECD designation of high quality but low equity (Robinson et al., 2011). The various international markers for this inequality have been the larger-than-average contributions of whānau, family, and student background to the differences between students in overall achievement in literacy.[11]

The international data are mirrored in many years' worth of national data collected in various formats, ranging from the patchy measures on entry to school through the short-lived National Standards, the ongoing various achievement test results, the various national monitoring projects, and the senior secondary qualifications. This is a long-lived as well as a long-standing blot on the excellence. It is why this chapter is about learning from some (but not all) children.

Te Kotahitanga

Russell Bishop has contributed significantly to righting this picture of excellence in learning being limited to some. He is a Māori researcher with a secondary teaching background, who developed a ground-breaking design for an intervention to increase engagement and achievement of Māori students in secondary schools mainly serving low-income families. It was designed to solve the low engagement of Māori students, starkly revealed in patterns of attendance and measures of students' sense of belonging. His idea is the second piece of evidence for learning from some children.

The Te Kotahitanga project (Bishop et al., 2009) showed that if teachers listened closely to the perceptions and recounts of their Māori students, profound changes could happen. Secondary teachers from different subject areas for Year 9 (14-year-old) and Year 10 (15-year-old) students would meet together to discuss the social, cultural, and academic needs of individual students, using their achievement and other

---

11 educationcounts.govt.nz/publications/series/PISA/pisa-2018

data. Their students' views on teaching and their lives in classrooms had been recorded and conveyed to their teachers, confronting them with insights—sometimes very challenging and uncomfortable—into how the students felt they were or weren't respected, and how they felt they were undervalued and given dumbed-down tasks.

This seemingly simple act of being ākonga-centred was associated with greater engagement by Māori students, and higher achievement in some areas. Admittedly, co-ordination of teachers' concerns for students and students' concerns about teachers across subject areas was just one component of a wider intervention. But it was the core component coming from an extraordinary insight. Māori students would be able to articulate why they were less engaged than their Pākehā peers. So the solution to what would be needed to increase their engagement and learning? Ask them! That is, learn from the children. Bishop and his team designed a programme that did exactly that.

Russell Bishop's intervention was not based on a detailed psychometric investigation of the validity of student voice. He had been an innovative and passionate teacher and, together with theorising about the nature of student agency and the lens afforded by Māori epistemology and practices, his was an insight that was spot on in intervention terms.

It turns out he was spot on in psychometric terms, too. Student voice has high predictive validity, as shown in the large-scale Measures of Effective Teaching (MET) project funded by the Gates Foundation.[12] Student perceptions can be at least as accurate as systematic observations of the quality of classroom teaching in predicting the value that a teacher adds to students' learning. Bishop knew students' views were critical to understanding how to solve the engagement problem. Many students told his team, in the first tranche of the research, that they felt they were given dumbed-down tasks, that the teachers didn't respect them, and that their views weren't listened to. Bishop's team shared these views with the teachers, in a very respectful way. They

---

12 https://usprogram.gatesfoundation.org/news-and-insights/articles/measures-of-effective-teaching-project, http://k12education.gatesfoundation.org/

shared (and helped mediate) them in the neutral but supportive space of the school marae, or if there wasn't one, a local marae.

Te Kotahitanga was an intervention project, funded by the New Zealand Ministry of Education. It received extensive evaluations. It was eventually rolled out to around 20 secondary schools. Like many intensive educational programmes, it showed that when implemented with high fidelity it was effective, especially for engagement in school. But like many educational programmes, the evidence also showed highly variable quality of implementation, and it proved difficult to scale up and make business as usual.

Both of these processes, variability and taking to scale, are fundamental challenges for educational science, and they proved particularly problematic for Te Kotahitanga. The programme needed to build the capability in schools to collect the data and to sustain the collective understanding of students, rather than these being provided by the external team. It was too expensive and, as Bishop found out, more was needed in leadership and pedagogy to leverage off the core process. These features of the programme meant that funding was discontinued for a time. Two iterations of the original project, using it as a proof of concept, have occurred. It has been resurrected in the form of a new design, Te Hurihanganui,[13] based on the evidence gleaned from the variable implementations and iterations that included leadership and instructional focus components.

Bishop's basic insight is what matters to the argument here. Like the Ready to Read books, Te Kotahitanga showed us the power of learning from the children themselves. Their voices must be at the heart of any intervention that makes a difference. His insight showed us how to include equity in excellence. It is to do with what we had been excellent in for a long time, but we needed to do it for all.

---

13 https://assets.education.govt.nz/public/Documents/our-work/Te-Hurihanganui/MOE19434-Te-Hurihunganui-Blueprint-4.pdf

System accommodating to some children

Aotearoa New Zealand is unusual in when our new entrants start school. They can have their first day at any time during the school year, having turned 5 years old. They are not legally required to be at school until 6 years, but our custom has been to allow a flexible start from 5 years. Up until recently, 90% of children did this.

It is hard to establish quite where or why this practice started. The most likely explanation is that in early small rural communities there was not a large number of children who could form a cohort for entry, say at the beginning or halfway through the year. Additionally, the teachers likely had children of their own and allowing them to come to school as early as possible solved a childcare problem. In the remote rural context it made sense for younger children to be at school.

Whatever the reason, it is well ingrained but currently perhaps under modification which could undermine this strength. It is argued that flexible start dates require the teacher of these new entrants to consider individual children on their own terms rather than as a member of a cohort who are defined on entry as similar. A typical practice has been to form a new entrant class with a small number of children, similar to a reception class in the United Kingdom, which increases in numbers until a point is reached and ongoing assessments indicate who might be promoted to a more formal Year 1 class. This is very obviously child-centred, because it would be easier and more manageable to have an intake once or twice a year.

The practice has been under threat more than once, and not just on pragmatic grounds. The prominent New Zealand researcher Warwick Elley, who led the first of the international (IEA) studies comparing countries' literacy achievement, queried the practice in 1992 (Elley, 1992). The data indicated that while we were in the top group of countries in the world for 9-year-olds, we were the only one that had this practice. The Scandinavian countries started formal schooling much later. In addition, there was evidence for a large gender gap. Elley wondered whether the flexible practice meant we were allowing boys to start too early and whether we should delay for a more formal cohort entry, especially for them.

Elley's critique did not hold sway. More recent attacks have come during reviews of the Education Act and reviews of the schooling sector. In each case the arguments have been more about schools being able to manage the transition better, and organisational needs. In each case they have fared no better than Elley's arguments did, although there are now more schools that manage the intake by grouping cohorts term-by-term. It is a deeply entrenched practice, which shows the needs of the child, and perhaps family needs, trumping organisational needs. But perhaps more importantly it epitomises this sense of treating each child on their own terms. It does, however, require a better evidence base. We need better data on how to make sure effective practices for all children are in place. And we need better resourcing to enable it to happen without stressing the organisation of the school. Finally, if we are to shift to a more managed entry, we need to know how to preserve the strengths of the existing practice.

Child-centred during COVID-19?

What would be the evidence for continuing this child-centred strength in our educational response to COVID-19 on children? The evidence would be that we responded to what children needed during lockdowns and, in the case of Tāmaki Makaurau Auckland, repeated lockdowns.

There are two ways of answering this question, which reflect two sorts of digital divides. The first digital divide—unequal access to digital infrastructure, connectivity, and quality devices—has been an issue in Aotearoa New Zealand and the COVID-19 period starkly reinforced it. We were very agile at delivering the Chromebooks, routers, wireless infrastructure, hard kits of educational materials, and educational TV that were missing (Dowden, 2022). But despite extraordinary agility, we only partly ameliorated the disparities. The rapid response to accessing broadband, wireless, and the infrastructure of digital technology reduced the disparities over the first lockdowns, but continuing issues for some remained, reflecting existing disparities or poverty, and living conditions (Hunia et al., 2020).

The agility, of course, does show in some senses how well the system responded to the needs of children and their whānau. However, the infrastructure issues have been largely a responsibility of agencies other than education and provide a weak test of being child-centred. It is the answer to a second question that is more telling.

A second digital divide occurs where there are less complex and less educationally relevant usage patterns by students from poorer and less privileged communities. Is there evidence that the curriculum as delivered was responsive to children and their learning? Did we deliver resources that showed we learned from children and were attuned to their needs?

It is too early to tell the full story after 2 years. But what evidence we have suggests the pandemic response over the first year didn't accentuate existing differences (Webber, 2021). Encouragingly, the evidence is more detailed and methodologically sound than in some other jurisdictions because it draws on repeated measures of actual achievement in reading, writing, and mathematics before and after the lockdowns and compares the trends with patterns over many years. Other jurisdictions have used teacher estimates, or summer patterns when schools are "out"—the former also reflecting teacher expectations and bias and the latter not reflecting the occurrence of distance teaching and learning.

The evidence is that the differences that were pre-existing in learning were not exaggerated, despite the issues with access and connectivity. Intriguingly, unlike other jurisdictions and unlike the very few places that can draw on repeated measures, reading achievement and maths achievement essentially didn't drop. There was little or no learning loss in these areas, but there was in writing. This likely reflects the delivery of more curriculum material and more opportunities to learn in reading and mathematics than in writing online.

In addition to this evidence, there are anecdotes that suggest we leveraged off this strength of being responsive to children, but as I note in the final chapter there is also evidence that we could have been better at making children and young people the centre of the educational response. One secondary school sent students home a few days before the lockdown and tested their systems and the design of their online learning and teaching. The infrastructure was largely effective. But the feedback from the students led to a radical change in pedagogical design. Without this personalising, it is likely the school would have done what tends to happen with the adoption of new technology in schools, such as happened with the adoption of interactive whiteboards.[14] In the absence of intensive professional learning and development these were typically used to deliver traditional didactic teaching, essentially sophisticated worksheets.

This secondary school didn't fall into that trap. In the COVID-19 case the trap would have been delivering a classroom "stand up and deliver" teacher lesson albeit now via Zoom. The students told the school what they wanted was resources that were "rewindable", say a 10-minute text or activity they could do and redo, and then have access to the teacher for question and answer and discussion in an online environment.

There are other examples. A cluster of low-SES schools well versed in online teaching and learning continued their personalised online engagement during the lockdowns in Auckland. They provide examples of digital resources with new activities on the digital platforms expertly tailored to the students of each class. Just how widely these examples reach is being investigated by the Ministry of Education as I write.

Unlike the picture using the reading, writing, and maths measures, we don't really have systematic achievement evidence for senior secondary school students sitting the standards-based National Certificates of Educational Achievement (NCEA) exams. On the one hand we know that the cohort of students who were disadvantaged by COVID-19 in their opportunities to learn—and had revised requirements for standards of passes required for university entrance did as well in their first year at tertiary as previous cohorts unaffected by COVID-19 (Universities New Zealand & NZQA, 2022). On the other hand, we also know that secondary students' wellbeing had been affected, with increased anxiety over the risks of not being as well prepared (Education Review Office, 2021). It appeared that overall loss

---

14   Discussed further in McNaughton (2018) and specifically reported in Hennessy & London (2013).

was likely to have happened, and exaggeration of that loss for already vulnerable groups was also likely. Being responsive at a system level to this potential learning loss and the anxiety, the criteria for passing and the crediting of standards were changed.[15]

Where did the strength of being child-centred come from?

The "from where" question can be repeated here too. Certainly, the international shifts to child-centred pedagogy were taken up in Aotearoa New Zealand by Beeby and others. But there is a strong tradition of caring for and considering children in our educational provisions. Anthropologists and historians have argued that being child-centred was a feature of precolonial childrearing. Anne Salmond's careful interrogation of records by early European visitors in the mid 17th and 18th centuries, including the French explorer Julien Crozet and the missionary Jean-Simon Barnard, leads to a picture of great affection, close protection, little if any physical punishment, and considerable indulgence. So much so, that this child-centredness offended the sensibilities of the standards of Victorian England (Salmond, 2018).

English sensibilities notwithstanding, another historical vein might be the focus on education that the colonial Scots brought with them. Charles II's concern for education of the young may have jumped time and lands and entered the mix. At first glance that explanation could be limited, being applicable possibly only to Dunedin, where Scottish settlers and their passion for education were most evident. But Scots settled in other parts of Aotearoa New Zealand and made up 30% of the UK-born immigrants between 1853 and 1870. There was a large settlement in Waipu north of Auckland settled by Scots via Nova Scotia.[16]

Scottish colonists, being almost a third of settlers over a 20-year period, coupled with the precolonial indigenous values and the push to literacy by Māori (detailed in the next chapter), may have helped to establish the child-centredness in education. But in some areas there

---

15 https://www2.nzqa.govt.nz/about-us/emergency-events/how-covid-19-affected-new-zealand-qualifications/

16 https://teara.govt.nz/en/scots/page-4

are historical limits to our being child-centred, especially those areas relating to physical and emotional risk. It took many years to ban corporal punishment from schools—it was in 1990, 20 years after Sweden. It took us 14 years to extend the requirement for drivers to wear seatbelts—mandated in 1975—to apply to children sitting in the back seat.

Despite an appalling record of farm accidents, a number of which involve children, we still haven't regulated the use of quad bikes on farms. In one District Health Board (Auckland), over a 7-year period, 27 under-16-year-olds with an average age below 10 years were admitted with injuries directly relating to quad bikes. Almost a third of them died. Helmets were being worn by only a third of the children in these cases (Pearce & Miles, 2015).

Paradoxically, there are constant gripes that our children are being too "mollycoddled" and that risk and danger are necessary ingredients for development to occur. Even now as I write there are renewed calls here and internationally to allow more risky play in early years education, sometimes made without careful consideration of all the evidence: just Google "bubble-wrapped kids" or "mollycoddling kids" and similar phrases. There are appeals to the authority of pop neuroscience and associated myths, surface readings of romantic philosophers such as Rousseau, and leaps of faith from correlations rather than established causes.[17] These miss the essential point about the nature of play and the nature of risk, and the need for guidance and structure—albeit at a discreet distance when needed—provided by socialisation agents (see the discussion in Little, 2020). Do we really want the high levels of child accidents and deaths to continue—the most shameful of which are our child violence statistics?

This darker side of our childrearing means this is not an across-the-board sense of valuing children. Where does that negative influence come from? One colonial influence might be the "man alone" narrative: the rugged individual who tames the land against all odds, getting hurt and, if all goes according to plan, becoming ever more resilient. This theme is in New Zealand fiction and as well as film (e.g., McCormick,

---

17 For example, Haidt & Paresky (2019); Wynn (2016).

1959; Read, 2006). This may intersect with a framing of gender stereotyping. The rugged man means toughening up children, especially boys. Another colonial influence may be through the enduring negative effects of that enterprise on Māori. The loss of land, identity, and interconnectedness has created intergenerational trauma and an undermining of positive socialisation practices (see Pihama et al., 2019). Not being focused on the physical, emotional, and psychological needs of children is not excused by that traumatic history but it is, at least in part, explained.

Chapter 4

Trying to be bicultural

Like the chapter on learning from *only some* children, the title for this strength is qualified. It refers to a state of trying to learn—not succeeding, as yet. This is to make a distinction between our progress and what is still left to achieve, despite what a system has been trying to do for decades. It is also meant to convey a struggle by Māori for cultural identity in a schooling system largely created by non-Māori.

I was reminded of the distinction while sitting on an international advisory committee for an intervention in schools serving Aboriginal and Torres Strait Islander communities in Australia. It was 10 years ago and part way through the intervention. The intervention involved developing leaders who could lead a staff with high expectations, able to incorporate and build on the resources represented in the local community, including cultural and language resources, which these children brought to school. It aimed to scale up a very successful model based on the extraordinary accomplishments of one Aboriginal school leader at one school. At a crucial mid-point meeting, observational data were being shared which showed that in some classrooms in remote and very remote areas there were representations and artefacts of the community and everyday life appearing on the classroom walls.

One of the Aboriginal researchers saw these data as very significant. Another of the advisory committee members, a leading Māori researcher, queried whether this was reason to celebrate. His concern was whether it could be seen as significant because it was like what we used to call *taha Māori* (literally the Māori side or perspective) in schools in Aotearoa New Zealand. This had often meant simple words on the wall, for example for counting up to 10, or simple language uses such as e noho (sit down) and e tū (stand up), or iconic pictures of geysers and such.

But taha Māori also often meant little change to the deep grammar of mainstream schooling and, the Māori researcher argued, was tokenistic. What is actually needed is changes to pedagogy that engender mutual respect between learner and teacher, and that capitalise on cultural values and practices, greater complexity and challenge in activities, well-designed local curricula, and overcoming community mistrust built up through generations as a legacy of colonial mistakes. The Aboriginal leader pushed back on this critique. He still saw this as significant, given what these Australian schools had been like previously. For these schools, he argued, it was significant progress.

What we have been good at in recent years is trying to be bicultural. We have gone some way beyond the window dressing about which my colleague was concerned. But the question is, how far and in what ways?

The relativity in the claim, however, begs the question of what are the indicators of being bicultural. The first three of five key indicators to me, as Pākehā, are the degree to which for Māori, the basic triumvirate of language, identity, and culture are accorded the same respect, consideration, and resourcing in schooling as their Treaty partners—tāngata Tiriti. The fourth indicator is schooling success. Whatever the valued metric of the day that defines the levels of success, we should be able to guarantee that Māori children and young people succeed with the same distributions of achievement levels as anyone else—the same percentage of high flyers, the same percentage of those who may need extra support—at every level of the schooling sector. The fifth is an issue primarily to do with Te Tiriti partners, the indicator being the commitment to being bilingual of tāngata Tiriti. How strong are our bicultural identities from the non-Māori partners?

We have made some progress in the first three indicators compared with the draconian colonial agenda of undermining cultural norms, values, and practices in schools—notably with the suppression of te reo Māori starting in 1867. The language ban was only gradually lifted and in a piecemeal fashion, starting with the denominational Māori boarding schools, and then when Māori was made an official language of New Zealand under the Māori Language Act 1987. Te reo Māori may be studied as an additional language in the curriculum and may also be the medium of instruction, across all learning areas. We have Māori-medium schooling and kura kaupapa Māori.

In terms of educational success, we have gone beyond the uncritical assumption that our ways of teaching and schooling are enlightened and world leading. However, clearly we have still quite a way to go. The schooling sector is more self-critical now, more attuned to the evidence and trying hard in the light of decades of evidence for our limited progress. We have yet to achieve the same honesty about what mainstream early childhood education is achieving for Māori, not just in access and participation but in terms of the basic indicators of success.

It is good that as a system we recognise our faults and build on successes. There is progress. But we need accelerated progress to be truly bicultural. Accelerated progress has several meanings. In terms of specific outcomes of schooling there is a technical meaning. Accelerated progress is needed, not to "close gaps", which is a limiting way of judging success. The measure of success, as I noted above, should be in the distributions of what is achieved. The distributions of skills and knowledge, success, and excellence valued by the curriculum should be at least the same for Māori as what is expected nationally for any student, and this may mean accelerating the teaching and learning.

There is a related meaning, which is the fourth indicator described above. Pathways through tertiary education and employment should be distributed similarly. Blunt outcomes such as a minimum agreed high school leaving level—as we had up until 2018 as a Better Public Service goal, set at NCEA Level 2 for most students—don't meet this meaning of success.

Finally, being bicultural should also mean becoming a citizen with the skills and knowledge sufficient to move between cultural worlds. Some will be very skilled and grounded in one cultural world or the other. But the everyday citizen should have the wherewithal to be competent in both. This is like being bilingual. It is a state of being able to shift between contexts and their practices, engaging successfully and with respect.

Education has a major role to play in this citizenship learning, and we are way better than we used to be. The primary school I went to on the outskirts of Hamilton was Forest Lake Primary. I don't remember anything Māori about that school apart from my best friend from up the road who was Māori. If one accesses the website for the school now, you see it has a Māori name, Te Kura o Roto Ngahere. It has a Māori welcome, a Māori representation of core school values, and Māori concepts are woven throughout the various windows in the drop-down menu. This is a long way from what it was like when I was there.

The examples that follow show how we are trying at various levels. They are concerned with the bicultural nature of schooling in Aotearoa New Zealand for tāngata Tiriti and iwi Māori. In trying to get this right we are also laying a foundation for being multicultural—an inclusive system which nevertheless enables distinctiveness for the communities that are adding to, and will come to add to, who we are.

Native Schools: An unlikely innovation hub for te reo Māori and culturally significant practices

The first example involves a paradox. It is the Native Schools set up by the colonial enterprise. Despite their purpose to colonise, they were also a vehicle for Māori impacting mainstream schooling. The following example of a remarkable form of peer tutoring—tuakana-teina relationships as business-as-usual in mainstream schooling—is traceable back to how some Native Schools provided a vehicle for a precolonial practice to be incorporated into schooling. It can be matched by other examples. One already described is the genesis in the Native Schools of the beginning reading series that replaced the colonially imposed Janet and John readers.

The Native School system was used to suppress te reo Māori, including with physical punishment for speakers, and it nearly succeeded. But even in this enterprise there were pockets of resistance and innovation that reflected a bicultural commitment. Here is a Pākehā teacher in the Native Schools during the 1930s talking about supporting te reo Māori:

> I used to get the senior girls to come down and give the little ones instructions and information in Māori. At first they used to say 'We don't know how', but they were just shy and very reticent to do that. So [we] were using the Māori language to facilitate. We didn't let on to the inspectors. They would just come in and stay for a day and look on and then we just said goodbye to them. (Simon et al., 2001, p. 98)

It turns out there are many examples of trying to be bicultural within business-as-usual in mainstream English-medium classrooms which it seems owe their presence to what some Native Schools enabled. "Seems" is used here because I can only draw connections rather than causal relationships, but the historical record is nevertheless compelling. One is what would generally and internationally be called peer tutoring. Schools have had a long tradition of using peer tutoring as an adjunct to teacher-led instruction, often in the form of cross-age tutoring within multi-age classrooms.

But one form of what looks like peer tutoring has greater significance than the international forms. It is expressed in terms of a traditional relationship in te ao Māori, and it is present and celebrated in English-medium schooling. It is called tuakana–teina. This relationship originally meant an older brother, sister, or cousin helping or guiding a younger sibling or cousin of the same gender. It is derived from the terms for older sibling (tuakana) and younger sibling (teina). It is closely related to another concept from te ao Māori, the concept of ako, which connotes flexible roles and commonalities between being a learner (ākonga) and being the teacher (kaiako). The practices of tuakana–teina reflect the dual nature of ako, which—when prefixes and suffixes are added to the root—can come to mean "to learn" as well as "to teach".

The evidence is that its route into mainstream schooling may have been through the Native Schools. There are many examples in the oral histories provided by Judith Simon and Linda Tuhiwai Smith in their book on the Native Schools. In the following quote, older children came to look after and directly teach younger children: "We found over the years that the best teachers ever in Māori schools were Māori children. You got the [older] children to help teach the younger ones" (Teacher 1947–1963) (Simon & Smith, 2001, p. 98).

Tuakana–teina has come to have a broader meaning in mainstream English-medium schooling, with older or more expert peers guiding younger, less expert peers. This practice is so much a part of our schooling culture that it is written into our curriculum guidelines and resources. For example, one of the key competencies valued in the curriculum is *relating to others*. Search Te Kete Ipurangi,[18] the online education resource hosted by the Ministry of Education, and you will find many references to peer tutoring (69 at my last count). But you will find 3,294 references to tuakana–teina.

And it is not limited to schooling. It is employed as part of the pedagogy in the early childhood sector. It can be found in the tertiary sector. At my university, Waipapa Taumata Rau University of Auckland, it is formalised in a significant university-wide mentoring and support community called the Tuākana programme, designed to enhance the academic success of Māori students and Pacific students.[19]

Not surprisingly, the wider empirical literature on peer tutoring substantiates the duality of ako. Under best conditions the tutor learns as well as the tutee; in essence, the tutee is also teaching the tutor through the progressive interactions. Drawing on the wider international literature, peer tutoring practices can be seen to reflect the concepts of duality in tutorial learning in Russian psychology. Under best conditions it puts in place what the Russian psychologist Lev Vygotsky called a Zone of Proximal Development (Vygotsky, 1978). We have included the practices in our national Best Evidence Synthesis

---

18   https://www.tki.org.nz/

19   https://www.auckland.ac.nz/en/creative/study-with-us/maori-and-pacific-students/tuakana-programme.html

research reviews. It was identified almost 20 years ago in the first of the Best Evidence Synthesis programme as a practice contributing to the dimensions of quality teaching for diverse students (Alton-Lee, 2003). Given its effect sizes it is seen as able to contribute to pedagogy which promotes learning orientations, student self-regulation, meta-cognitive strategies, and thoughtful student discourse.

Teachers moved into and out of the Native Schools system. My assumption is that the recognition of the strength of tuakana–teina from the Native Schools impacted patterns in the English-medium schools. Following at a distance this became embedded and then we provided the cultural rationales and the rationales from educational sciences. Developmental and educational psychology often follow behind and seek to understand what has become innovative practice in schools, and this is a powerful example.

The rise of kōhanga reo, kura kaupapa Māori, and wānanga

In 1977 a series of meetings was held in Wellington (see Rei & Hamon, 1993). Convened by Kara Puketapu, the head of what was then the Department of Māori Affairs, iwi leaders came together to address a singular concern: the imminent demise of te reo Māori. Iritana Tāwhiwhirangi, the charismatic long-serving head of Te Kōhanga Reo Trust, called what followed "organic". The iwi leaders, old and young, men and women, came to solve a looming crisis.

Their concern was also evidence-based. A Pākehā researcher, Richard Benton, began a survey 4 years earlier that ultimately was to take 5 years (Benton, 1973). It was the first sociolinguistic survey of te reo Māori and it helped create the tipping point in the fate of the language. The survey, known as the Benton Report, gathered information from 33,338 individuals in 6,470 whānau throughout the North Island.

The exercise was a "lean operation". With extraordinary commitment, interviews were done kanohi ki te kanohi (face-to-face) and with no dedicated funding. Benton was to describe his findings to the Waitangi Tribunal as showing that the expectation that the language would survive, even in heartland villages outside of the main centres, was "not realistic".

The organic groundswell and the cold facts helped galvanise people, and the first language nest, Te Kōhanga Reo, opened in Pukeatua, Wainuiomata, in April 1982. By 2018 there were 450 kōhanga reo in Aotearoa, attended by approximately 17% of Māori children enrolled in early childhood education services. Te Kōhanga Reo became the largest employer of Māori women in the early learning sector, employing approximately 2,250 women and training 750 women each year. The supporting infrastructure is well established, with a Trust and approved training courses leading to recognised qualifications.

Te Kōhanga Reo created a parallel early learning system to the existing system. But as their graduates moved into primary school it became readily apparent that tamariki were at risk of losing what they had gained. Primary immersion schools with a guiding Māori philosophy, kura kaupapa Māori, were then established. The first of these, Te Kura Kaupapa Māori o Hoani Waititi, emerged in Auckland in 1985.[20] As with Te Kōhanga Reo, in the early stages whānau were forced to fundraise to run their kura until they received government recognition and funding. Kura kaupapa Māori gained recognition in the Education Act 1989 and from 1990 the Ministry of Education supported the establishment of new kura. Secondary schools soon followed. There is now a tertiary system of recognised tertiary providers and universities. Three wānanga are recognised under the Education and Training Act 2020 as universities: Te Whare Wānanga o Awanuiārangi, Te Wānanga o Aotearoa, and Te Wānanga o Raukawa. There have been further developments of Māori frameworks and foci leading to two bodies with constellations of kura: Ngā-Kura-ā-Iwi and Te Rūnanga Nui o Ngā Kura Kaupapa Māori.

This is a diverse system which sits alongside the English-medium system. It has legislative recognition in all its sectors; there is an early learning curriculum and a primary and secondary curriculum which are not just translations of the English medium but purpose-built, by

---

20 https://teara.govt.nz/en/maori-education-matauranga/print

and for Māori. What is most important is that detailed analyses show ākonga attending these schools through to secondary levels achieve significantly better at the senior exams than Māori students in the English-medium schools (Mhuru, 2019). It is on these measures of achievement and of language regeneration that this parallel system can be called an outstanding success. But in terms of physical and educational resources and infrastructure, by comparison with the mainstream system it is not well off and still vulnerable to being discriminated against, requiring constant battling for equity.[21]

There is a risk of course with parallel systems, that they may become siloed. The risk, all too often experienced, is that the Māori system can be left to its own resources or its needs considered as an afterthought after new resources and support are provided to the English-medium state school system, illustrated by the constant battling for recognition and resources. The English-medium public school system faces different stresses, but a critical one relates to one of the criteria I proposed above. It is a telling metric—the degree to which the dominating system is responding to the need to be bicultural.

Other system indicators: The curriculum, and learning te reo Māori

Tuakana–teina tutoring is a powerful but limited example of learning to be bicultural in the English-medium public school system. Are there others? A meeting with a kaumātua more than a quarter of a century ago, when I was doing research work with colleagues at another university, provided an early indication of where we might look. He was the kaumātua for the university's Department of Education, following a stellar career in educational roles including as an inspector of schools. I heard him speak several times of a visit that had clearly impressed him. It was to a remote school serving high country farming families. The children at the school were all Pākehā. He was met at the gate of the school with a rousing haka performed by a well-drilled kapa haka

---

21 For example, the ongoing claim to the Waitangi tribunal from Te Runanga Nui o Nga Kura Kaupapa Māori, Wai 1718. https://forms.justice.govt.nz/search/Documents/WT/wt_DOC_191156240/Wai%201718%2C%203.1.032.pdf

group. His delight was in the presence, through the New Zealand curriculum, of practices with which he identified.

The criticism by the Māori educator I described earlier could still be applied, that this and the example from my primary school could be seen as the window dressing of taha Māori. So what is the state of us being bicultural now, as judged by what's in the English-medium curriculum?

As I rewrote this section following the start of COVID-19 there were protests around the world under the banner "Black Lives Matter". In the United Kingdom, alumni of the top-tier public schools called on their schools to incorporate texts from Black writers into their curriculum and more generally to decolonise the canon and develop a more critical curriculum (Speare-Cole, 2020).

Our history of being bicultural is far from perfect. The 2014 survey finding noted earlier that only a quarter of Year 4 and Year 8 students reported they had read texts that reflect their culture and identity (by Year 8 only 16%) suggests that imperfection in terms of opportunities for mirror texts.[22] Unfortunately, the 2014 survey didn't provide a breakdown by ethnicity. But a repeat of the assessment cycle for English achievement in 2019 reported on an item which asked students whether they had opportunities to link what they read to what happens in their lives. A third of Māori students at Year 4 and a quarter at Year 8 reported "never".[23] These data are reflected in other surveys which probe Māori students' feelings of being discriminated against, or valued, or that they belong at school.[24]

The simple comparisons around reading are worrying. They are supported by evidence further up the school system. The canon of texts in English studied by high school students for many years has included Māori writers such as Witi Ihimaera and Patricia Grace, as well as Pacific writers such as Albert Wendt. So they are "in", but this begs the question of how valued they might be.

---

22 https://nmssa-production.s3.amazonaws.com/documents/Reading_SOF.pdf
23 https://shiny-uat.nzcer.org.nz/nationalmonitoring/2019/
24 Examples: Jang-Jones & McGregor (2019); McGregor & Webber (2019).

The standards-based senior exams mean that specific standards provide evidence of what students have studied in preparation for the exams. For example in 2021, at Level 1 NCEA (typically 16-year-olds) the standard 90849 (now 91925) required students to show that they understand specific aspects of a text they have studied. What students chose to write about for this standard reflected choices of their teachers, including on what texts they can best show their understanding. Public assessment reports that were available from recent years showed the usual examples of Western fiction. More accurately, writers from the United Kingdom and United States were typically chosen: *Of Mice and Men*, *Animal Farm*, *To Kill a Mockingbird*, *Nineteen Eighty-Four*, *Montana 1948*, *Lord of the Flies*, and war poetry; there were fewer examples of Māori texts. There is an equivalent standard for visual texts and, pleasingly, Māori images and themes are more present in those texts studied, with movies such as *Dark Horse* being in the list of popular choices.

Learning in te reo Māori is another indicator. The Ministry of Education definition of Māori-medium education is that at least 51% of the curriculum is delivered in te reo Māori. On this definition just under 3% of the total school population is in Māori medium. The percentage of students who are learning te reo Māori as a subject or are receiving up to 50% of the curriculum in Māori (and that can be less than 3 hours a week) is 22%, and notably more non-Māori (64%) than Māori students have been in these provisions. Of the three-quarters of the school population not engaged in any form of Māori medium, close to two-thirds (60%) are likely experiencing taha Māori, what was referenced earlier as potentially tokenistic: simple words, greetings, or songs in Māori. This breakdown starkly shows the "trying to be" condition. At a system level, the bright but sometimes faltering light is the growth of fully Māori education.

The presence of mātauranga Māori (literally Māori knowledge) in the current curriculum refresh process perfectly illustrates the system trying to be bicultural and learning how (and how not) to do that.

> Mātauranga Māori will sit at the heart of the learning areas …
> This will help ākonga understand a dynamic and evolving knowledge system unique to Aotearoa.²⁵

The need for mātauranga is perhaps most obvious in Aotearoa New Zealand's histories in the refreshed Social Sciences learning area, which requires our children to learn how histories are created and by whom, and key content of those histories. It has become more contentious in the process of refreshing the Science curriculum. A small group of academics viewed this as denigrating science because indigenous knowledge is "not science", generating widespread debate, some of it well informed and some not so well informed (Clements et al., 2021).

Understanding a system trying to learn is in some ways like understanding children's learning and subsequent development. We can use different time-frames, ranging from the broad sweep of a life course down to micro-level learning in real time. We learn in the acts of perceiving patterns, responding to perturbations in what we know and do, drawing connections, forming and testing ideas, making errors and correcting. The role of tutorial supports to scaffold the acts, especially early on in the learning, is fundamental. Under the ideal conditions, what eventuates can be progressively increasing knowledge and skill.

The science curriculum-refresh process has been and continues to be contentious because of the vision to sit mātauranga Māori centrally. Mistakes have been made, such as not making visible in early drafts core non-negotiable content and knowledge in the sciences. A very significant issue, given the high-level nature of our curricula, is having the capability in classrooms to enact the nuances in the curriculum. This means understanding and teaching how and where knowledge systems relate and don't relate, and their place in understanding our

---

25 https://curriculumrefresh.education.govt.nz/whats-changing

world. Thankfully, we have very knowledgeable and skilful tutors who are helping to scaffold, our capabilities.[26]

From where?

Why try to be bicultural? There is a powerful demonstration from Māori of what being bicultural could mean, both before and after signing Te Tiriti o Waitangi. It is the rapid acquisition of literacy, an indicator like so many others of what Māori have brought to the partnership table. The evidence shows that more Māori than European settlers were literate very early on in the colonial history. Māori quickly learned to read and write, in part to learn about Christianity but more so to understand, use, and adapt European technology for a variety of purposes including correspondence. Māori appeared to acquire scriptural literacy easily within the missionary schools and then within their villages. The Catholic missionary Bishop Pompallier believed that Māori could read within 3 months "as they would persevere endlessly with slates in hand". Māori eagerly taught other Māori, helping to spread the novelty of literacy and the Gospel. Newspapers by Māori appeared (Jones & Jenkins, 2011; Warren, 2015).

George Clarke, a missionary and the "Chief Protector of Aborigines", one of many egregious colonial titles, observed from his travels through Waikato and Hauraki in the late 1840s that there was a Māori-run school in nearly every village he visited.[27] By the early 1840s, it is estimated half of the adult Māori population was able to read and write in English to some extent.

The last example tells much of the story. Tāngata whenua, and some parts of the colonial powers, laid the foundation. There is the official platform provided by the founding document of Te Tiriti o Waitangi. The Treaty is a broad statement of principles between two peoples, with an English and Māori version. The Crown and many Māori tribes

---

26 Two examples are the Māori academics writing about science and knowledge systems in Kukutai et al., (2021) and those by the Prime Minister's Chief Science Advisor and others on the interface: https://www.pmcsa.ac.nz/2019/12/19/matauranga-and-science/

27 https://teara.govt.nz/en/maori-education-matauranga/page-2

agreed to act in accordance with the principles on how to live together as a nation. The document has three articles. In the English version, Māori cede the sovereignty to Britain and give the Crown the right to buy lands they wish to sell. In return, Māori are guaranteed full rights of ownership of their lands, forests, fisheries, and other possessions, and gain the rights and privileges of British subjects. In the Māori version, the three articles use concepts of kawanatanga (the right to govern is given to the Crown but tribes retain the right to manage their own affairs), tino rangatiratanga (tribes are promised full authority over their lands and taonga and resources including the language—te reo Māori), and ōritetanga (partners have equal rights). Presumably the colonial education requirement to use English and to ban Māori in schools was in breach of one if not all three articles.

Our history shows that the Treaty principles were interpreted differently and held different meanings in the two versions. More significantly, they were conveniently ignored or forgotten by non-Māori and successive Governments. It was Māori who kept the commitment alive and, after many decades, in the 1970s forced the Crown to honour the Treaty and hold the Crown accountable. The Waitangi Tribunal, created in 1995, is the embodiment of an agreement to honour the principles of two peoples being together.

So one part of the press to be bicultural was a founding document and a commitment over many years by one of the partners. Less formal roots can be found in the deep intercultural relationships within and between families and whānau.[28] There was understanding of and resistance by some Pākehā teachers to the damaging elements of colonial education, but that begs the question about where their awareness and commitment to change came from. I have earlier reviewed some of the evidence from the Native Schools (Simon & Smith, 2001). But to add contemporary voices, there are those from two academics, one a sociologist and the other a behavioural psychologist, who have been writing about the why and how from a Pākehā perspective (Glynn, 2021; Jones, 2020). Ted Glynn's awareness and need to act came from

---

28 Many of us identify with more than one ethnic group and the figure is high for Māori: https://www.stats.govt.nz/tools/2018-census-ethnic-group-summaries/māori

several sources. Notably, these were family connections with Ngāti Porou through a stepbrother, and family history. It also came from his leading role in studies of educational change and learning of the stark results of systemic racism. There was also a strong sense of outrage at oppression, which he attributes to his Irish background.

For Alison Jones it was close experiences with Māori friends at school, an acute awareness of place and position as Pākehā in Aotearoa New Zealand, a similar outrage at the inequalities exposed through her experiences as an academic, her radicalisation through feminist ideology and action, and her learning from Māori activists.

These two academics see learning to be bicultural for Pākehā as coming to grips with the realities of the past, but also being forward-looking as contributors to the promises of the Treaty. It also involves becoming (bi)culturally competent, with personal relationships and more formal partnerships mirroring those anticipated in the Treaty. Not surprisingly, for both academics, education is key.

These voices suggest the central role of intercultural experiences, present at the beginning of the colonial contact and in individuals' everyday lives as we construct and remodel our identities. Te Tiriti o Waitangi | The Treaty of Waitangi is a clear point of reference. But there is also the resilience and cultural norms and practices of Māori and a predilection to solve, resist, or co-opt rather than succumb.

Chapter 5
Having partnerships

I learned a powerful lesson about the roles and responsibilities within educational partnerships early in our research programme to support local "low-decile" schools increase their effectiveness. We had developed very good processes in a partnership model similar to what has been called continuous improvement, or improvement science (Lai et al., 2020). In our case, through the early 2000s we were developing our ideas for research and development methods in education called design-based interventions. A number of models for education were being developed around this time. We called ours the Learning Schools Model (LSM), emphasising that schools were learning, and we were learning from the schools.

One component was setting shared goals for success and using systematically collected evidence to judge success against those goals. The processes we developed meant that there were regular meaning-making sessions with our partners, often the leaders in the schools. These hui, which involved feedback and joint problem solving using the shared evidence, were very important.

At one such hui we presented data on the achievement levels the schools were reaching. I enthusiastically presented graphs and tables showing in essence that the average achievement levels were close to nationally expected levels. This was undeniably a very significant outcome both educationally and statistically speaking.

The partnership included the schools' Boards of Trustees. Each school in Aotearoa New Zealand is governed by a Board and the combined Boards of several schools in the district were represented in a Boards Forum. The chairperson, a member of the local Pacific community, was present. He responded to my presentation with a challenge. "Stuart," he said, "We don't want our children to be just average."

This challenge led me to new ways of thinking about how to judge educational success. I learned it is not enough to close gaps, in the rhetoric of the day. It is not enough to reach the average. Rather, the gold standard for success, as I have argued in previous chapters, has to be one of equitable distributions of success. That is, students from Māori communities, Pacific communities, or from low-SES communities have the right to the same distribution of success as would be expected nationally—that is, the same proportion of students in the top bands of the most successful, the same proportion in the bottom bands with the same slice of low achievement, and the same bunch in the middle. Nothing more or less should suffice. This was his message to me. The partnership was the vehicle for my learning, and it reminded me of the strength of partnerships. As with the other strengths, the significance of partnerships can be seen at various levels of the system, the first at the beginning of children's formal schooling.

Hearing reading at home

Learning to read in Aotearoa New Zealand involves a local partnership of a special sort, between the teachers in the early years and the family and whānau of the children learning to read. Since at least 1962 a practice of sending books home for a family member to hear their child read has occurred. It was conceived by the then Department of Education as a "close working relationship", and became universally embedded in primary schools (McNaughton et al., 1992).

Various programmes for supporting the practices at home have been designed. One I was involved in developing and testing was entitled Pause, Prompt, and Praise. It travelled offshore and was used in both the United Kingdom and Australia. It also was redesigned for use in Māori immersion contexts as Tatari, Tautoko, Tauawhi (Berryman et al., 1995). It has been repurposed into a peer tutoring form and, with added language, into a programme that is used in early childhood as well as up into the middle primary years called Reading Together.[29]

Over decades, experimental studies have shown that the practice adds to children's learning. The studies have identified the conditions for its effectiveness, which include information being shared between settings of home and classroom, and clear guidance for family members in how to "hear" children reading orally. The evidence for the significance of this close local arrangement is consistent. It is associated with some of the largest effect sizes for simple early reading interventions (Robinson et al., 2009).

But the practice should not be confused with homework. It doesn't have the same features. It is designed to be a joint practice. It is at its best a partnership or collaboration which, given the design of the early text readers and careful preparation by teachers, and the condition of appropriate guidance noted earlier, is engaging—for both the reader and the family member. It is a practice with which all children in a classroom can engage, and able to be adjusted to the level of difficulty of the text being read. It is designed to show children at their best, as teachers send books that children can read and family members are responding to their expertise rather than to deficits.

This system of individual systems comprised of a teacher or more expert person and the child is what the developmental psychologist Urie Bronfenbrenner called a "mesosystem" (Bronfenbrenner, 1979). It functions effectively when information is shared, there are joint goals, and the interaction patterns are complementary. This universal feature of early learning in schools is a strength, a classroom-level prototypical educational partnership.

Collaborative problem solving

There are partnerships of note at other levels. Our students are good at collaborative problem solving. Several sources of evidence show this. Recent PISA studies tested collaborative problem solving on

---

[29] https://www.readingtogether.net.nz/reading-together-research.html

computers (working with others to solve a problem through a shared understanding and group focus) in a game-based format. It turns out this was a strength of Aotearoa New Zealand's 15-year-olds (May, 2017). Our students do this very well, better than all the countries in the OECD study bar one; an educational success that is not acknowledged as much as other features in the international comparisons.

This strength is all the more compelling against the backdrop of the lowering scores in other international comparisons, specifically in reading (Progress in International Reading Literacy Study, PIRLS; Programme for International Student Assessment, PISA), science, and mathematics (Trends in International Mathematics and Science Study, TIMSS). We were once in the top group of countries on these comparisons, reflecting the sorts of literacy practices I have outlined which coalesced around a pivot point in the early 1960s. But at an aggregated level we are getting worse at reading literacy, science literacy, and maths literacy. The reasons for the drops are not the subject of this book and are dealt with elsewhere (McNaughton, 2002, 2023). Suffice to say the solution to the drops, specifically in literacy, can be found in some of the ways proposed in the last chapter in this book.

This strength in having partners, the collaborative skills of students, may be related to the finding that our students also score relatively highly in evaluating and designing scientific enquiry (May, 2019). Subject knowledge contributes to achievement in subjects such as science, but collaborative skills that are generalisable across subjects also contribute and have been found to be more important, statistically speaking, than ethnicity and SES to collective scientific enquiry in schools. The power of these student partnerships is indicated in how being collective adds value to individual limitations in subject knowledge and skills.

However, the evidence also shows that this excellence is as susceptible as any other area of schooling to inherent patterns of bias and inequitable resources. Unfortunately, the equity challenges are present in these excellent data on collaborating around problems, and graphically illustrate the challenge I was faced with to think beyond averages. The percentage of Māori or Pacific 15-year-olds in the highest achievement bands for collaborative problem solving is less than half that of other groups, and conversely in the lowest achievement bands is much more than double other groups. A similar pattern is found for the students from the families that have the lowest access to financial, educational, and social resources.

Relationships and collaboration between schools

Regrettably, despite this strength, we have limited collaboration at the less granular level of between schools. This is the result of a major system design flaw, which has finally been found wanting. Paradoxically, the flaw came about because we prioritised one sort of partnership over another.

The educational policy producing this paradox has resulted in a natural experiment. In 1989, a radical form of local school governance was put in place. The Tomorrow's Schools policy created self-governing schools, autonomous local units, with control ceded to a local Board of Trustees elected from the local community for each school. The idea of this "local democracy" was visionary, and had an evidence base and an explicit values base. The design rationale specifically drew on the strength derived from collaboration between a school and its local community.

Strengthening this relationship through the governance of the school was meant to formalise the benefits that could flow from direct community involvement. There would be a local school charter that the community produced, that reflected the values and aspirations of the community. An empowered community would engage in the everyday life of the school and the sense of collective responsibility would increase the value of education for all participants and the relevance of decision making. If it worked well it would create the mesosystem I referred to above, a system of linked powerful "microsystems" that are the basic units fostering a child's development. To the degree these systems are well co-ordinated and mutually informative, the developmental potential of each of the embedded systems would be enhanced.

Many parents at the time reported a sense of excitement and real responsibility working on the school charter and engaging with the school. Unfortunately, the great idea had an unintended consequence. It reduced collaboration between schools. Not only that, it increased competition. The evidence is that both "white" and "brown" flight occurred, and strong well-resourced schools became stronger. These outcomes happened because the local autonomous schools were islands, susceptible to limitations in local resources—a system-level example of ubiquitous Matthew effects (the rich get richer) in education (Ministry of Education, 2018).

The rest of Bronfenbrenner's ecological model of development had been ignored. The school and families and whānau in the mesosystem are embedded in a larger system of neighbourhoods and community resources. These provide enablers and constraints on the mesosystem and ultimately the child in their microsystems. Local infrastructure, transport, green spaces, libraries, amenities, liquor stores, and fast food outlets and the like matter to children's learning. And these "exosystems" in turn are embedded like Russian dolls in a wider system of systems, an overarching "macrosystem" of policy making, ideologies, beliefs, and values, which determine the everyday lives of children and whānau such as housing policies, employment practices, and resourcing to schools. Without policy settings which underpinned mutually supportive and sustained collaboration between schools, the unintended consequences flowed. We didn't account for differential access to knowledge and funding that Boards of Trustees from different communities might have, and we didn't adjust funding and resourcing to schools sufficiently to reduce inequalities.

New designs have been developed. In characteristic fashion the new designs are not mandatory. The Kāhui Ako or Communities of Learning were designed to increase collaboration between schools. They were also supposed to increase hapū/iwi engagement. Like many interventions or changes implemented nationally, it has had varying degrees of success. New roles have been developed for within-school and between-school leadership. This leadership is to function as the mechanism to increase teachers within and between schools learning from each other. Early evidence is that this has happened although with our characteristic variability.

The natural experiment creating autonomous schools illustrates the strength of partnerships. Redesigning to create networks of schools is also an illustration of the strength. The two deliberate design interventions were both driven by a focus on collaboration: on one hand, the collaboration between the school and its community, and on the other, collaboration between local or like schools.

Collaborations between research and policy

There have been productive partnerships between policy makers and researchers, through which local research has informed policy with long periods of collaboration.

I was once asked by an eminent Professor of Education at Harvard why her colleague, who had spent some time in Aotearoa New Zealand, had had so much influence on local educational policy thinking. One reason was that her colleague was a very skilled researcher, committed to learning from local conditions—a key component of being an effective partner. She made it a priority to collaborate on the ground with local researchers and spent time with them in schools and in community settings, responding to these communities with respect and humility.

Another more parochial explanation is New Zealand's version of the 6 degrees of separation. We are a small, closely related population and there is more like 1.5 degrees of separation between any one researcher and any one policy person. This means it is very easy to connect, and establish commonalities. Surprisingly often, there are families/whānau, friends, work, or locations that are common to the potential partners. This means it is possible to simply phone, text, or in other ways establish contact and build partnerships. The international researcher and her collaborators easily connected with policy colleagues, and her research-based evidence became powerful, especially in thinking about the nature of classroom discourse for Māori and Pasifika students.

The research impact arises in part from the skills that the visiting academic from Harvard had. She had skills of connecting and forming partnerships, which are not necessarily common among academics. In addition, the few degrees of separation mean that these skills, or sadly different influential skills such as wielding charisma and authority rather than mutuality, can impact educational decision making at a school or wider level.

There are other examples. There was a long-standing collaboration between researchers, educators, and policy makers in the research and development programme that led to Reading Recovery, a world-leading early intervention for literacy learning. The partnership wasn't built on charisma or appeals to authority, but on the careful and robust science of the day, and on the mutually respectful and informative relationships between the researchers, practitioners, and educational policy colleagues (Clay, 2007). The partnership was the basis for the national implementation through the Ministry of Education.

A collaboration of sorts around Reading Recovery has been in place for over 20 years, surviving successive Governments and government commissions into literacy achievement.[30] But, like many educational collaborations, it has lessened. Becoming "business as usual" has meant less joint redesign and development, and more of a contractual relationship. This is changing in the light of new evidence and new foci. A redesign to be better fit-for-purpose for current and future needs is underway. Once again, this is involving close collaboration and problem solving between partners.

An up-to-date example of the science and policy making collaboration is the formation of the system of science advisors (of which I have been a member). Distinguished Professor Sir Peter Gluckman

---

30 I note for a potential conflict of interest that I am a Trustee of the Marie Clay Literacy Trust, a trust set up by the researcher who designed Reading Recovery. The charitable trust exists to promote literacy in Aotearoa New Zealand, and through the royalties it receives from sale of books is able to fund research and support local academics (through prizes and scholarships) and educators (through support for travel). It has a relationship with the international bodies that implement Reading Recovery but has no direct control over the procedures and the implementation of the intervention.

established the initial role of Chief Science Advisor to the Prime Minister. A group of science advisors was then established in each of the major agencies. Sir Peter's successor, Professor Dame Juliet Gerrard, has broadened and diversified the group. The significance of this relationship has been on display all through the COVID-19 period, in the foreground as science advisors for health. Their networks provided advice which needed to be dynamic as we learned more about the pandemic. But also in the background, advisors have collaborated with their agencies around evidence-informed responses, including providing evidence about the needs of whānau, families, and children for wellbeing when in lockdown conditions.

Why?

It is tempting, as in other areas, to go to our cultural strengths. Tāngata whenua cultural practices include the traditional forms of collectivism. As I have noted already, Māori collective responsibilities were obviously present early in the colonial enterprise in the Native Schools. The accounts from oral histories identify instances of the archetypal familial relationships present in schools, built on reciprocal responsibilities between older and younger members of a family, but adapted to older or more expert students having reciprocal relationships with younger or less expert peers.

The original tuakana–teina whānau-based relationship led to the well-established forms of cross-age tutoring described earlier. It is present at all levels of the educational system. At Waipapa Taumata Rau University of Auckland, the tuakana–teina relationship is the basis for the highly effective support systems for Māori and Pasifika students. In addition, there may be a generalised influence from other practices from te ao Māori. Making connections between individuals and groups is central to formal speech-making (whaikōrero) in the rituals of the marae, and this important mahi hononga (connection work) lies at the heart of Māori interactions more generally.

The evidence for the existence of nascent collaborative strength in schools, drawn from Māori communities and through the Native Schools, is strong. However, the ever-present inequalities, for example in the collaborative problem-solving data, mean some nuancing in the explanation is needed. Poverty, poor housing, and lack of access to financial and educational resources play a part, and diminish cultural strengths if schools are not well designed to overcome the out-of-school factors. This is especially so because academic achievement in the areas of school-related problem solving plays a significant part. This means that it is most likely that these relationship strengths have been or are being dampened down, filtered out, or interfered with. Systemic racism and intended or unintended discrimination also reduce engagement and potential development of the school applications of collaboration present in the community.

Did the colonial partners to Te Tiriti o Waitangi add to this strength? At first glance that seems unlikely, given a view of Western individualism. However, we need to go beyond simplified psychological models of cultures, which identify cultures as (only) collectivist and (only) individualistic. Māori in this naïve binary are quintessentially collectivist. But there is a more complex cultural narrative in the creationist stories that celebrate the role of the entrepreneurial individual, such as the demigod Maui. Individuality is present but with deep responsibility to the collective for what they know and achieve and can pass on.

On the other hand, the representation of Western cultures as quintessentially individualistic needs to be nuanced too. Collectivity and extended family responsibilities are present in the history of Gaelic Scotland and Ireland. Many Scots and Irish families arrived very early in the colonial era. But there is a complexity here too. A counter to the simple view of adding collectivist Gaelic practices are the farming narratives, in written text and in film described earlier. They lean on the "man alone" motif and his struggle with the bush and the elements. There is not much collaborating in that motif.

But, despite these narratives and their tensions, the colonial experience may turn out to be a further source. The colonial experience contained many elements of collectivism and co-operation, both brought with colonists and through the need in farming, despite the narrative, to succeed in a foreign, perhaps imposing land.

A parochial example of the cultural expression of being connected that does cut across cultural groups can be overheard when Kiwis first meet. It may be in a foreign place, often in the overseas experience part of many Kiwis' lives, or just at a local event or venue. Often the conversation starts with the question "Where are you from?", very quickly followed up with "Do you know x?". The need to make connections and establish relationships is keenly felt.

Chapter 6

Creativity and innovation

A leading Māori researcher told me the following story about being creative. He was newly graduated from what was at the time Auckland Teachers' Training College. His first posting was to a local intermediate school. Despite his newness, the principal of that school gave him the task of identifying gifted and talented students to provide extension activities for them.

The literature on identifying and selecting gifted students is fraught. Should we look for students who are generally gifted across many areas, or those who are highly talented in one area? Should we pull individuals out and try to personalise their education even more, go fast (accelerated progress), or go wide (extension within the cohort)?

A telling feature in many models of gifted and talented students is that they are creative. My friend, being who he was, had an ingenious (and indigenous) creative solution to this challenge. He went to the kapa haka group, the group largely Māori who were learning waiata and haka at the school, and chose them en masse for the gifted and talented programme. His argument was that being Māori and creative was a pretty good indicator!

Having a go

Fred Dagg was a character created by one of our funniest and most successful comedians. The character was a farmer, wearing a black singlet, longish tatty shorts, gumboots, and a floppy hat. Fred Dagg, John Clarke's alter ego, solved stuff (and also mercilessly parodied Government policies). He made creative use of whatever was around. In one comic episode he made use of the then Government's newly devised "sheep retention" scheme. The sheep retention scheme was a lever the Government used to reverse the drop in sheep numbers (as subsidies to sheep farmers were removed in the early 1970s) by paying farmers to retain sheep. Fred's solution was to engage in "retenting", finding non-existent sheep and creatively counting them and, in another anarchic act of creativity, stapling fleeces back on to sheep in an invented process called "woolling" because the fleeces weren't selling (no animals were hurt in this episode!).

The idea of New Zealanders having a go, often with wild and wacky schemes, is a well-rehearsed trope. It is most universally represented as solving with "number 8 wire", the wire used to fence paddocks. This wire could be used for many purposes. I heard a famous cartoonist using a version of this idea when entertaining audiences with family stories. He used the refrain "You never know when they will come in handy," relating to things his father would collect and not throw out. The most bizarre and seemingly useless things were held on to. Old saucers from the cups and saucers that the New Zealand Railways Corporation, when it was state owned, provided to long-distance travellers were bought as a job lot by his father. The cartoonist's refrain, after each story of a purchase, was to repeat what his father would say: "You never know when they will come in handy." Number 8 wire and its many uses figured prominently.

The funniest part of the presentation was that fully three-quarters of the audience had the same experience and repeated the refrain with gusto. My mother would say that. Using everyday objects for inventive and unusual purposes is a hallmark of creativity and a response to living with limited resources, and these anecdotes suggest it is widespread—at least in my and previous generations.

The question is whether such creativity is present and could be seen as a strength in our educational system. Much of what has been written under the earlier themes could be seen as creative. The early reading books were created by many teachers rejecting long-held practices. The integrated curriculum based on artistic expression developed by Elwyn Richardson is by definition a creative enterprise. Certainly, the expectation is that teachers will create local curricula centred on students, as has been repeatedly observed in previous chapters.

The basic structures for what to teach invite creativity. In literacy pedagogy it wasn't until 2003 that specific reference to what constituted deliberate acts of teaching in literacy was made (in the national resource *Effective Literacy Practice in Years 1–4*).[31] A framework of evidence-informed instructional practices such as feedback, prompting, and modelling was outlined. But there was still the expectation that teaching involved using these acts on an as-needed basis, as fit for the purpose at hand. Rather than assuming, as some commentaries might lead you to think, that teaching always involves providing highly informative feedback, the expectation was that feedback is used when needed for this student, at this time, on this task.

But is creativity deeply embedded and does it matter in education? Perhaps a better way to phrase the first part of the question is whether creativity bursts out under conducive conditions. The answer to that is yes. Examples can be found both early in our educational history and contemporaneously. It seems we have always been at least a little creative.

Digital Learning Objects in classrooms

Who would have thought that the new digital tools in schools could be used for creativity? Not only can they, they may be redefining the nature of creativity. Contrary to the not-so-pretty picture of an engrossed individual learner intent on problem solving or constructing, is one of a similarly engrossed but playful creator, often working with others, virtually.

Our research team discovered this somewhat after the fact when studying schools where the evidence showed the pedagogy that

---

31 https://literacyonline.tki.org.nz/Literacy-Online/Planning-for-my-students-needs/Effective-Literacy-Practice-Years-1-4

included creativity had a very significant impact on achievement in writing (Jesson et al., 2018). Teachers in the groups of urban and rural low-decile schools called Manaiakalani schools, whose children were steeped in the use of their own digital devices, had figured this out with their students. The technical term is utilising the "affordances" of the tools. The teachers and students had realised that one of the affordances of one's own computer, linked into a classroom dashboard, with archiving functions and a range of editing and presentation tools, was to enable the creation of Digital Learning Objects (DLOs) which could be shared with others within and outside the classroom. In maths, for example, the problem could become a centrepiece embellished with cunningly presented solutions. The critical commentary in English could use hyperlinked clips, animation sequences, and multimodal presentations, the learner acting with an online presence as a producer of knowledge.

Being a designer and producer is required in learner-created digital learning artefacts, such as mash-up and remix designs and other multimodal creations. This does not mean core skills are being sacrificed. For example, in these schools writing skills are being learned at an accelerated pace. The reason? The component skills of writing to produce a DLO are being learned and deliberately practised within the activity of creation: an awareness of audience, organisation of text, structured and logical development of ideas, use of sentence variety, and precise choices of vocabulary.

School level creativity: Pockets of promise

Digital innovation is present in clusters of schools. I know one example very well because our research team spent years evaluating and helping build the innovation through close analysis of what was (and wasn't) working well and optimising the large-scale take up across schools.

The innovation is typical of what we do in Aotearoa New Zealand, and exemplifies other themes such as being local. Leaders who had devoted much of their professional lives to the equity challenge in schools serving communities with limited access to social, economic, and educational resources saw the potential in early adoption of digital tools. It came to be known as Manaiakalani (the Hook of Heaven), the name made up of Māori and Pasifika concepts.

Manaiakalani schools have been very successful in many different ways. With partners they have enabled communities with the lowest employment and income levels to rent-to-own digital devices. They capitalised on what the Google suite of tools provides for teachers. They have successfully coordinated telcos to make sure the communities have super-fast broadband and wireless connectivity. The schools used a partnership model, which is novel in international terms, to engage with our team of researchers who helped inform and energise their continuous improvement cycles.

One can be creative without being effective. Innovation doesn't always lead to success, however defined. Many people start small businesses; the survival rate after several years drops below 50%.[32] In the case of Manaiakalani, however, the schools' innovation is a deal breaker. The schools have been able to raise writing achievement as well as reading and mathematics by impressive amounts (Jesson et al, 2018a; 2018b). Accelerating rates of learning in these schools is a resource-intense, long-term commitment and they have proved to be champions. Unlike many small businesses, over 10 years the Manaiakalani design has not only survived, but has been successfully scaled up to around a 100 schools from the original nine.

But Manaiakalani schools illustrate an educational challenge that we have not been so good at solving. There are very few examples where a great idea that is creative, innovative, and effective has been taken to scale. Apart from Manaiakalani, the examples range from Reading Recovery created in the 1970s through to the School Journals created in the early 1900s. Sometimes this weakness in taking to scale has been because the idea proved ineffective or because it petered out with changes in leaders or the original creators. Sometimes it was a limitation of its own making, proving to be not cost-effective in its original form, or proving hard to take to scale because it was so dependent on the designers and the initial resourcing.

---

32 https://www.mbie.govt.nz/assets/small-business-factsheet-2021.pdf

This matter of creativity sustained and at scale is something we are not good at. It is also the Achilles' heel of being local and a limitation in our forms of collaboration. How to take a great idea, which is successful and cost effective, beyond the local? I have written about this as one of the core challenges of the educational system elsewhere, and I will explore it a little further in the last chapter.

National creativity: The School Journals

It turns out that creativity was present early in the colonial days of schooling. It was in the form of creative anthologies of books. Not only that, but like the identification of kapa haka as a selection device for gifted and talented students, it had Māori dimensions.

In 1907 a remarkable publication from the (then) Department of Education was launched, not without controversy (O'Brien, 2007).[33] This was the start of the School Journals, the year New Zealand became a dominion. Over more than 110 years, 7- to 14-year-olds have been able to access, free of charge, a compendium or anthology series of prose, poetry, reports, drama, and other hybrid texts. Access was a right, and the books had impact. There are accounts of children in remote Māori communities eagerly anticipating the delivery of the journals (Simon & Smith, 2001).

What is remarkable is that it started with locally written prose pieces, but also retellings of Māori creationist stories, and even retellings of classic European fables in local forms. Over the years it has deliberately become more and more local. It exemplifies the themes we have already discussed of what we are good at: being local, being child-centred, and trying to be bicultural.

But even more remarkable is who has written and illustrated the Journals. It has been a vehicle for and enabler of national creativity. Many of our most creative writers and artists have written and illustrated the Journals: literary icons such as Witi Ihimaera, Margaret Mahy, Joy Cowley, Elsie Locke, James K. Baxter, Patricia Grace, Janet Frame, Alistair Te Ariki Campbell, Brian Sutton-Smith, Conrad Frieboe,

---

33 For a readable account, see White (2017).

Juliet Peter, Rita Angus, Dick Frizzell, Gavin Bishop, Lani Young, Gus Sinaumea Hunter, and others. It is a long and illustrious list.

It is one thing to launch a creative enterprise. It is another to protect it and grow it in the face of resistance. The launch, as I noted, was not without controversy. At the beginning voices were raised about the local content being a literary travesty, shades of more recent feedback over attempting to put local writing into the English curriculum, or local history into the Social Sciences curriculum. As it became more local, the voices continued to be raised against the use of colloquial language and popular themes and representations. More recently, as we look back at the material with more clarity and understanding, we have realised that much was written with a very Eurocentric lens, and in places is simply racist.

But the School Journal has survived. The urge to be creative has been strong. Even with the change from its original home in the school publications branch of the (then) Department of Education to a state-owned enterprise, a partly privatised entity charged with making a profit for the Minister of Education, and then to a fully privatised company the free, local, and creative urge has been protected and has prevailed.

National creativity: A bigger picture

Even more general examples of national creativity can be identified. The examples range from radical new designs for the system as a whole through to the creation of completely new curricula.

Clarence Beeby became the Director of Education in 1940. Over 20 years he created a radically remodelled educational system which shifted towards a broad, balanced, and equitable system that was children-centred. This visionary architect abolished the Proficiency Exam which had restricted access to secondary education; instituted a process of teacher judgment via accreditation for entrance to university; introduced a school leaving qualification to recognise the skills and knowledge of all students, especially those not wishing to go on to further study; and developed kindergarten and other preschool early learning services as a partnership between the state and voluntary organisations.

It seems unremarkable now to consider an early learning curriculum a creative artefact. But it was remarkable when it was designed in 1993, if the criteria include being innovative and world-leading, and entailing divergent thinking as a liberal progressive/socially critical document within a "neo-liberal and neo-conservative" political climate (Mutch, 2004). The Ministry of Education subsequently published the fully fledged early childhood curriculum *Te Whāriki* in 1996. It was updated 20 years later to better reflect, among other things, a stronger bicultural emphasis with a focus on identity, language, and culture, and more specific and fewer learning outcomes, reflecting the theme of being child-centred but addressing the tension in being too loose with the expectations (Ministry of Education, 2017a, 2017b)).

The development of Boards of Trustees was creative against these criteria too. As I have noted, it had unintended negative consequences. But if the action of completely remodelling a system and having a go at designing something unique fits the description of being creative, it was certainly that. These are examples of a system prepared to be creative and to innovate.

Reflections post COVID-19

Responses to COVID-19 have showcased creativity in the education sector. But perhaps the most blatant example comes from an unlikely sector, the advertising industry. Ads have been created aimed at social messaging. The most recent through the COVID-19 period was aimed at keeping children safe from online pornography. It used naked porn actors.

Earlier ads had been designed to combat foetal alcohol disorder and drugged driving (directed by international film director Taika Waititi). Each are described as drawing heavily on a uniquely Kiwi humorous streak and are recognised as both creative in international terms and very engaging (Fastnedge, 2020). The ad directed at keeping children safe from online pornography had, by early July 2020, 25 million views.

The ad to combat foetal alcohol syndrome became YouTube's most successful public awareness campaign in Australia and New Zealand.

We don't always get these ads right, as examples from the safety videos on Air New Zealand flights sometimes show. But commentators attribute the success of New Zealand ads, at least those in the social impact area, to a combination of small budgets, tighter agency–client relationships, and the creative sense of humour (Fastnedge, 2020).

The creativity during the various phases of the response to the pandemic was not confined to the advertising industry. There are many examples of innovation and creativity in education. I described in Chapter 3 the response of a secondary school who tested their online connectivity and capability. The school's innovation came in what they did with the results. They listened to their students' feedback and redesigned their pedagogy (being child-centred). Rather than one-hour lessons, they created "rewindable" resources which the teacher could put online and which students could download and work on in their own time. The time for the "lesson" was used for online dialogue or conferencing.

This school discovered by themselves what had already been discovered in another set of schools—the ones I wrote about earlier, the low-SES Manaiakalani schools that had been innovating with digital devices and tools for some years. They had worked out that using the tools in ways that gave more agency to the students with digital artefacts, hyperlinked bundles of texts, and rewindable resources was key. It made real the promise of the tools as having affordance for increased learner agency, but it meant that the teachers functioned even more as curriculum and pedagogical design experts with the digital tools, ensuring a rich curriculum delivered digitally.

This use of technology is a far cry from some of the romantic naivety around digital online learning, which sees the technology freeing up students from the shackles of neoliberal forms of mechanical mass production. It can redefine the student's agency in pace, sequence, timing, and even content of learning. But it redefines the teacher, too. The affordances are for teachers also being more agentive, being even more adaptive and expert in local curriculum design, and being creative with online resources. This was the nature of the school's innovation, a school seen from the outside as typifying traditional didactic forms of pedagogy.

Our examples in Aotearoa New Zealand of being able to rapidly shift to generative forms of online learning, or in some cases extend the hybrid forms of learning and teaching already in place, is remarkable in international terms. In one 2013 study of the adoption of interactive whiteboards, teachers in the OECD countries largely used them as more powerful forms of worksheets (Hennessy & London, 2013). That study estimated that it would take an extended period of professional development time, measured in months not days, to change the beliefs, perceptions, and practised ways of teaching to better utilise what the interactive tool enabled.

There are many other examples from the COVID-19 period. They range across the education sector from early learning to tertiary. They include teachers and students creating new resources and new platforms, as well as whānau in partnership with teachers creatively adapting to teaching and learning at home.[34] These examples are an antidote to the usual simple narrative about communities that traditionally have not been well served by schooling being "vulnerable".[35]

The traditional high-SES school discovered and changed their pedagogy in a matter of hours. The country moved to the new or redesigned forms over very few days with a mixture of rapid rollout of devices, online resources to schools, a new educational television channel, and a hard pack delivered to those in communities with low connectivity. We didn't get it consistently right and the very agility uncovered the inequalities. The digital divides became very obvious,

---

34 See examples of creativity, innovation, adaptability and resilience here:
    https://www.auckland.ac.nz/en/news/2020/07/10/innovation-meets-education.html
    https://www.auckland.ac.nz/en/news/2020/09/24/Locked-down-but-not-locked-out-of-learning.html

35 For examples of creativity, innovation, adaptability, and resilience, see Hunia et al., 2020; Enari & Matapo, 2020.

as the Ministry of Education's evaluation of their response revealed (Dowden, 2022).

Why?

So why might we be good at this? This is where the "man alone'" and associated themes of getting stuck in and solving something might be applicable. Edmund Hillary "knocking the bugger off" plays into that image. But of course, as Hillary acknowledged, that was achieved through a group effort.

Pākehā colonists may have brought a pragmatic problem-solving attitude. But narratives about being creative problems solvers already present in te ao Māori contributed too. The creationist stories of the demigod Maui are rich in celebrating the creative genius of an individual, the difference being in the motivations for and responsibilities going with the creativity. The individual's creativity is motivated by, reflects, and builds on the collective's needs and aspirations. The genius creator has responsibility to make the contribution on behalf of others. Maui tames the sun for the sake of the tribe. Maui fishes up Aotearoa New Zealand, against the wishes of his brothers, for ngā iwi katoa.

Real leaders are also celebrated for their creativity. It is recorded that Te Rauparaha, the chief who composed the famous haka "Ka Mate" while hiding from enemies, is also famous for deciding to learn to read and then requiring his whole tribe to learn. The adoption of new tools (for example, by acquiring muskets then carving their stocks with traditional Māori patterns) and the invention of trench warfare are also examples of local innovation (Belich, 1998).

Each of these observations suggests we have valued and supported innovation and creativity in pre- and postcolonial times. This may be the source of the creativity we value in teaching and schools.

Chapter 7
Not being good enough

Being relatively strong in five broad features of education is laudable, but could these strengths make a difference where it counts, to better meet our excellence and equity outcomes? One way to answer that question is to look for the evidence base that these attributes are important to educational system outcomes. I have introduced some evidence in previous chapters and review more of that evidence in what follows.

Another way to answer the question is to ask about the counterfactual. Could we be even worse in our excellence and equity performance if we didn't have a child-centred approach, if we weren't design experts in local curricula, if we ignored educationally important connections, steadfastly remained monocultural, and were boring? If we didn't have the strengths, where would we be on the equity and excellence metrics?

It turns out that the evidence is clear and that considering the counterfactuals shows we would be notably less effective compared with what we currently try to do. The problem isn't with these strengths and with the evidence for these being strengths. The problem with our current limitations lies elsewhere.

Not good enough for equity, mixed for excellence

But let's start with laying out the evidence, challenged by the bad news. Clearly, the five broad features have not been sufficient to solve the enduring problem of inequality in our overall educational success. They have not been sufficient to arrest declines in some of the quality indicators (undermining our overall high quality), such as the fall in achievement in 15-year-olds' reading, science and maths, starting around 2009, or what the OECD calls our "bleak" bullying rates.[36] Does this mean they are interesting, but essentially epiphenomena? Or worse, that one or more of them stops us from being successful, as a recent report from a local think tank argues.

Learning from children

The New Zealand Initiative (NZI), a think tank which grew out of the New Zealand Business Roundtable, recently claimed that our child-centred strength, learning from children, is worse than a 21st distraction (Lipson, 2020). It has "ruined a once world-leading school system". Why would that be?

One reason the NZI report offers is an appeal to cognitive science which, so the report argues, leads to the conclusion that the singular focus of teaching should be on valued content; it should be knowledge-rich. Furthermore, being child-centred (i.e., learning from children) has had two inappropriate effects: differentiating instruction to suit individual learners, and placing more control over what is learned in the hands of the learner, both of which undermine effective instruction.

Contrary to the NZI claim, each of these is firmly based on evidence from cognitive science (and the encompassing field of the science of learning; see Darling-Hammond, 2020). A core principle from cognitive sciences is for instruction to "start where the learner is at", including their current knowledge base, which means not treating all learners the same. It actually does mean differentiating the instruction. Very

---

36 https://www.auckland.ac.nz/en/creative/study-with-us/maori-and-pacific-students/tuakana-programme.html

effective instruction depends on having a detailed and comprehensive understanding of a learner's cognitive strengths and needs, and teaching to these. We have systematic experimental evidence about this.

A simple example from one component of beginning literacy instruction is that differentiated instruction is needed in early phonics teaching (Puzio et al., 2020). Children start school with varying understanding of the alphabetic system and with varying levels of phonological knowledge and phonemic awareness. Some children will need quite detailed systematic phonics instruction, while others will need much less, so time spent in detailed explicit instruction would interfere with their learning of other components.

Despite the weak argument and selective use of evidence in the NZI report, it does cause us to pause and think. Perhaps being child-centred carries risks? It does, if we don't get learning from children right. Quite rightly, the NZI report turns to a glaring example of not getting it right. The NZI report equates child-centred with pedagogical approaches such as inquiry and discovery learning in mathematics and science. To be clear, the evidence is strong. Pure inquiry or pure discovery really are less effective than didactic teaching in maths and science, both in terms of overall achievement and in terms of more variable learning (McNaughton, 2018). But there is rarely such a thing as the pure form, except in experimental tests under controlled conditions. Imagine the potential damage caused to life, limb, and property if pure inquiry into the thermite reaction was to occur in a school laboratory! However, there are everyday classroom examples that supply the evidence.

In ineffective classrooms, the pedagogy is strong on a superficial form of inquiry, weak on systematic guidance, and well-developed content knowledge is not available on which to draw. Conversely and not surprisingly, inquiry *plus* guided teaching—which, among other things, establishes needed content—is much more effective than direct teaching alone (reviewed in McNaughton, 2018).

Discovery and inquiry approaches conceived as relatively "hands off" teaching are misguided, as is teaching metacognition (awareness of one's knowledge and thoughts) without cognitions. The latter was a tendency in the United States after the discovery of metacognition in the 1970s by Anne Brown and others. Again, not surprisingly, we quickly learned that if you don't have much of anything concrete to think about, no amount of teaching about a process such as thinking about your understanding or critical thinking is going to make a difference.

To continue the bad news about inquiry, Aotearoa New Zealand has one of the highest rates of inquiry pedagogy in science classrooms across the OECD, and like the OECD generally, this is correlated with *lower* achievement in science (Kirkham, 2016). There are indications that the problem may be one of content knowledge. Our 15-year-olds rate their knowledge of environmental science topics lower than OECD averages in some cases (Ministry of Education, 2019). It is understandable from the point of view of the local curriculum why that might be the case for nuclear waste, but it is less clear why that should be true for climate change or for water quality, topics which are pressing concerns in many local areas.

Should the explanations for this include the general inappropriateness of being child-centred? Some years ago, the cognitive psychologist David Olson (2003) also argued that child-centred approaches had failed, but for a very different reason from the NZI report. He argues that it was not because schools adopting the approaches were wrong in principle, but because the child-centred narrative at the level of a school or classroom can be used as a rationale for just about any teaching practice.

The best explanation for the failure of inquiry approaches, apart from little or no guidance, and lack of requisite knowledge to inquire about, is how the curriculum is implemented. It is how the general theme of learning from children in science is taken by each teacher and enacted on the ground day by day, and how it is not as good as it should be. We know that we have problems in the sheer amount of time devoted to science, especially in primary schools, and in the content knowledge and confidence of teachers to teach science, and it is likely we have privileged the process of inquiry over the needed content. In this sense the NZI is right to challenge process domination. But their report was wrong to see this as a problem of learning from children (being child-centred).

There are threats to our strength of being child-centred, which were emerging before COVID-19. They are the calls to have inflexible instructional programmes in place, off-the-shelf prescriptions for how and what to teach. An example is how advocacy groups that provide professional development claim that the "science of reading" shows that their explicit, deliberate, highly prescribed approaches to teaching phonics, such as structured phonics, should be taught to all children beginning to learn to read and write, irrespective of children's existing levels of phonemic awareness and phonological and alphabetic knowledge, and in a lock-step fashion before real reading and writing for meaning and with intentionality and pleasure.[37] This is despite the evidence for the added value from differentiated instruction; the actual neuroscientific evidence about brain functioning and the role of non-linear neural networks, rather than rigid sequences assumed by formulaic structured approaches; and the evidence that adopting these views has not led to the valued outcomes, especially equity outcomes (Ellis & Bloch, 2021; Compton-Lilly et al., 2020; Wyse & Bradbury, 2022).

The counterfactual to consider is what would our system be like if we treated all children as if they were cognitively, socially, and emotionally the same; if teachers were technicians delivering a highly prescribed curriculum at all levels; and if learners were positioned as docile (i.e., non-agentive) consumers of content knowledge?

Clearly this is a hypothetical, because we can't do the experiment and set up control groups. But we can in some senses ask the question in a quasi-experimental way by looking for contrasting groups and cases. What do systems like that achieve? What happens when teachers and schools that were highly constrained with externally imposed quality assurance and prescribed curricula change?

There is some evidence to answer these questions. As is typical with such complex open problems, there isn't one dimension or universal

---

[37] https://www.liftingliteracyaotearoa.org.nz/initiatives/manifest

expression, often because culture and history in the local context shape that expression. But common principles can be detected. One of the dominant and generalisable themes is about teachers being highly skilled at differentiating instruction on the basis of detailed evidence about individuals, able to adapt to and learn from learners' needs and modify their instruction with evidence, with professional forms of accountability and learning rather than high prescription (OECD, 2018; Robinson et al., 2011; Schleicher, 2018). The counterfactual can be seen in microcosm in highly segregated tracked systems where students are selected as similar and treated as similar, resulting in highly unequal outcomes. The value added by student voice or agency increasingly figures in these analyses.

It is crucial we get even better at being child-centred. The solution to solving the equity challenges is to recognise and build the adaptive expertise of all teachers so as to be better at being child-centred. In turn, this requires being even better at being local.

Being local

What about being local? I can use the NZI report again as an introduction to thinking about whether this is a good thing or not. The report claimed that children should gain knowledge defined by a limited set of important things to know, specifically rejecting the idea of the local curriculum. This has been posed in the curriculum debates as debates over the "canon", the clear superiority of Eurocentric content versus the less significant local rest. The very revealing example used in the NZI report is pitting knowing something about the world's seven continents against knowing something about tītī (muttonbirds), the former being what should be valued.

But local knowledge is not antagonistic with the broader internationally valued knowledge of the sort referenced in the report. As I was writing this book the eminent Winton Professor of the Public Understanding of Risk at Oxford, David Spiegelhalter, made the claim I described in Chapter 2. The claim is that our teaching of statistics is the best in the world. In his view the New Zealand curriculum focus on statistics, which is larger than some other countries, plus our pedagogical design, has meant we are world leaders (Spiegelhalter, 2019). Our approach is problem-based, using local or arresting familiar examples as the problem to act on.

As I noted, this claim is cause for some local pride and feeds into the proposal to see being local as a strength. But the picture is complicated when one considers the patterns of actual achievement. In terms of achievement, our students in upper primary and secondary are better at statistics than they are at other branches of mathematics, in particular algebra and geometry (Ministry of Education, 2022). But we are by no means the best or even in the top group of countries in terms of achievement data, even for statistics.

Spiegelhalter was making a "best practice" claim. It is not sufficient to have a strength in best practice terms. It matters how we deliver the curriculum, enacting it on a daily basis and over the long haul. What it tells us also is that we may have good intentions and being local may be the way to go, but we have yet to solve the problem of how to make that strength work for all—the problem of achieving best practice at scale.

The challenge for teachers is to draw universal and robust knowledge out of the particular which is embodied in local knowledge, then to use the particular as the springboard to the general concepts and principles. It is a difficult challenge because the teacher has to know the general principles and concepts as well as the local instances. The teacher also needs to know how to join the two, using their pedagogical skills. Any one of these steps poses challenges for the teacher's pedagogical and child-centred knowledge, their decision making, and their strategies for teaching. In all, it is a punishingly difficult exercise in judgement.

It is especially hard to do in the context of culturally embedded knowledge and frames of reference for that knowledge. The challenge is captured beautifully in the short story *Butterflies* by the Māori writer Patricia Grace.[38] Proud grandparents send their loved granddaughter to school, where she is doing well at writing stories. When she gets home to their farm they ask about her day. She says that she

---

38 'Butterflies' in *Electric City and Other Stories*, Penguin, 1987.

has written a story. They are keen to hear it. She has written that she killed butterflies, and the grandparents ask what the teacher thought of it. She replies that the teacher was critical, saying that butterflies are "beautiful creatures" which fly in the sun and "visit pretty flowers". The teacher had also said that one does not kill butterflies. The grandfather then remarks that this is because she buys her cabbages from the supermarket.

Nevertheless, the criticism again gives us pause. Do we actually have the evidence that being local makes a difference? And the counterfactual, would we be worse if we weren't? In a word, yes. There is plenty of evidence to add to the research reviewed earlier. In areas as diverse as using mirror texts and culturally familiar images and language patterns to increase reading comprehension, through to the use of word problems in mathematics, embedding the problem to solve or the activity to engage in matters (Lee, 2007; Verschaffel et al., 2020). The local context, if it is really local and part of the learner's event knowledge, greatly aids successful solving and learning, at least in the short term.

But again, there are risks if we don't get it right. One risk already mentioned is the expertise of the teacher. Other risks include making assumptions about the learner's knowledge based on stereotypes or biases (see McNaughton, 2018, for a review of the evidence). There is also dependency on the familiar context and limited transfer or application to new and unfamiliar contexts. Mirror texts (in which one can see oneself and one's familiar context) need to be complemented by window texts, where one sees what is unfamiliar, metaphorically looking out to new worlds. Most recently there has been a wide-ranging critique that argues most word problems used in maths assessments do not reflect the real events and experiences of many children, and authenticity matters. That makes the point about being local even stronger.

Following the examples of our teaching history used earlier, the evidence is that we are better at being local in some of the areas we value than in others. Notably, we are also better at being local in our provisions for literacy learning but less so and with more variability in science, or in the social and emotional areas. Again, the issue isn't whether being local is a good thing; the issue has to do with capitalising on that strength.

There is a coda to this evaluation. Having been through years of COVID-19 experiences we have realised how important it is to understand local conditions. The lessons were learned not in curriculum terms but in terms of delivery of resources to tamariki and their families and whānau. The centralised information about where resources such as digital devices and access to the internet were needed was not sufficient. Using local community organisations such as those associated with the schools, community groups, or iwi turned out to be a much better route (Hunia et al., 2020).

This book is about what we are good at in education and whether we should leverage off those strengths to be even better. The current curriculum "refresh" is making it more explicit how to be local, which is cause for optimism about being better. Critically, it is very apparent that being better in this feature will require greater recognition of the status and significance of teaching, which is one of the conditions needed for being better, discussed further below.

Importantly, one expression of being local is the bourgeoning partnerships the Ministry of Education has with iwi (see, for example, Ministry of Education, 2021b). The aspiration for these is set in *Ka Hikitia—Ka Hāpaitia*, the Māori Education Strategy. Going beyond aspiration, the partnerships are developing in several areas, and with different degrees of formality. There are high level partnership agreements such as the Kawenata to establish a Tiriti/Treaty-based partnership based on equity and rangatiratanga, establishing a future of mana motuhake (self-determination).

Te Mataaho-a-Iwi is a formal partnership between iwi leaders and the Ministry of Education to provide iwi decision making with fit-for-purpose data and statistics. Less formal is the recognition that the curriculum refresh for Aotearoa New Zealand's histories requires access to local histories, with a process of funded collaborative design development happening to develop critical local histories.

But as the next strength exemplifies, there is much to do to ensure these partnerships adequately reflect the principles in Te Tiriti, and that the aspirations deliver on the promises. The recent claim made to the Waitangi Tribunal (Wai 1718) by Te Rūnanga Nui o Ngā Kura Kaupapa Māori is a powerful demonstration. The claim is that the Ministry of Education and the Crown hadn't honoured the principles by which kura kaupapa Māori should be run, failing to adequately resource, support, and promote kura kaupapa Māori.

Trying to be bicultural

The gap between the progress education has made in trying to be bicultural and in achieving success, fulfilling our obligations to be Te Tiriti/Treaty-led, is still quite large. As I pointed out in Chapter 4, this is not only a question of pedagogy and curriculum as such; it is a question also of commitment to deep values of respect and partnership. But it raises the gnarly question of why we haven't been more successful. Our statistics in education continue to show a seemingly intractable difficulty in creating an education system that is fully just and guarantees equitable success for two communities: tāngata whenua and tauiwi. Is this "trying to be bicultural" not a strength?

We know that the answer is not one for education alone. The answer requires further collective actions to solve the legacies of colonialism. This means delivering across agencies of national and local government—from housing to health—the resources that eliminate overt and unconscious discriminations in poverty, in justice, in social welfare, in living conditions, and in political power.

Having said that, education has a central role to play. In addition to being a Treaty obligation and a moral imperative to account for the colonial past, being bicultural directly affects schooling success. The galling thing is that we know how we could do it better in education. A major enabler of Māori achievement is living in a whānau with strong Māori identity, language, and culture (Ministry of Education, 2020c). This circumstance is highly predictive of success in our senior secondary national examinations, NCEA Level 2 and University Entrance. Attending Māori-medium schools increases the odds of achievement even more. Finally, a major impact on achievement is having teachers who are Māori. Even in English-medium secondary schools, if there are high numbers of Māori teachers, student achievement is higher. It is in these data that we can get a sense of the counterfactual; we would be even worse in our equity outcomes if we were not committed to becoming ever more bicultural.

These are not the only enablers, and some of those that derive from being Māori can be acted on in English-medium schooling. In Chapter 3 I reviewed the success of innovations in English-medium schooling such as the Te Kotahitanga project. That, together with other local research, is consistent with much of the international evidence, identifying a number of enablers for impacting engagement through to valued outcomes of achievement and wellbeing.[39] In English medium these include relationships of respect; differentiated and personalised instruction; an enacted curriculum driven by high expectations; pedagogy that is at the same time culturally responsive and of high generic quality; close community relationships; the use of local evidence and problem solving to support greater effectiveness; and leadership which sets a clear and compelling collective purpose focused on all of the above.[40] What makes a difference is the presence of non-Māori teachers who are committed to learning with and alongside Māori students and the communities they carry on their shoulders to school with them every day.

These are some of the elements we already know about. So again, we have evidence of the significance, and we also have evidence of what works, so why have we still got such a long way to go to resolve the equity issues associated with Māori achievement?

---

39 The recent OECD commentary on the education system recommends exactly this: spreading best practice from Kaupapa Māori and Māori medium pathways to the English medium pathway https://www.oecd-ilibrary.org/economics/oecd-economic-surveys-new-zealand-2024_603809f2-en

40 It is beyond the scope of this book to review all the relevant research here: recent international summaries include Darling-Hammond et al, (2020); local summaries can be found in the Best Evidence Synthesis resources https://www.educationcounts.govt.nz/topics/bes; and the programme of funded research through the Teaching and Learning Research Initiative http://www.tlri.org.nz

Updating this section through the COVID years I am more optimistic than I have ever been about further progress. We have discovered there are levers we can pull to improve the system. Some of these are already having an effect. The curriculum refresh that was beginning when I first started writing this book is advanced and Aotearoa New Zealand's histories is a reality; it was released in the week that I was re-editing this section (Ministry of Education, n.d.). Its themes require teachers to understand the core colonial and post-colonial experiences from Māori perspectives.

Making the bicultural understanding of our histories mandatory is not the only lever that has been used. It is accompanied by a requirement from the Teaching Council that all teachers from early learning through to those in secondary schooling must declare that they are developing and practising te reo and tikanga in order to renew their annual practising certificate. The requirements for demonstrating this are now explicit (Education Council, 2017).

Another lever further up the system could be used, one of the few that impacts university research. The Performance-Based Research Fund (PBRF) is the mechanism government uses to fund universities and it has been based on a 5-yearly audit of the excellence of research being conducted. Academic staff have their portfolios assessed and universities receive funding commensurate with the levels of excellence demonstrated. A recent review proposed that the weighting for mātauranga Māori research be increased to receive a higher rating than the most expensive sciences, the net result of which would be for universities and research programmes to more aggressively recognise, promote, and sustain Māori scholarship.[41] PBRF is now part of a wider review of the university sector, but the very act of proposing this illustrates the point about what levers are available.[42]

Overarching each of these and others—such as the increase in government support for Māori-medium education, kapa haka expertise recognised in credits for University Entrance, and formal partnerships

---

[41] https://www.tec.govt.nz/funding/funding-and-performance/funding/fund-finder/pbrf/

[42] https://uag.org.nz/

between the Ministry of Education and iwi to set resourcing and foci—reflects a more direct and explicit focus coming from the Ministry of Education. The government's Education Portfolio Work Programme[43] explicitly sets out to solve systemic inequalities. In 2020 a cross-agency strategy for Māori success was finalised. All the major sector groups have signed up to it.

Paradoxically, the negative reaction from some quarters to these shifts in the levers adds to my optimism. A very small but vocal group of academics has challenged the legitimacy of a bicultural framing of the curriculum and specifically for the science curriculum, sensing that the long-held privileging of what has been the default is under threat (Gerritsen, 2021; Dunlop, 2021; Sachedeva, 2021; Freshwater, 2021). A comment from the overarching body for universities, Universities New Zealand, suggested the PBRF proposal could "dilute science". Subsequently an apology for the unfortunate choice of words was issued. Similarly, Waipapa Taumata Rau University of Auckland, from where most of the small group of academics came, issued a very public statement distancing itself and asserting the institution's commitment to mātauranga Māori. The dialogue illustrated two very important outcomes related to our trying to be bicultural. It made the issues public, including our biases, both unintended and intended. Secondly, it made public a shared sense of the direction of change, illustrated by proposals for what a science system that understood and capitalised on mātauranga Māori could look like (Kukutai et al., 2021).

Relationships and collaboration

There is plenty of evidence that relationships matter to educational success. Just consider the counterfactual, "What would it look like if we had standalone schools who remained aloof from their communities?" At each of the levels reviewed in Chapter 4, do the relationships matter? Is our form of local democracy—self-managing schools with a Board of Trustees made up from the local community—a positive? Is the practice

---

43 https://www.education.govt.nz/our-work/information-releases/issue-specific-releases/education-portfolio-work-programme/

of sending books home adding value to both children and their families and whānau?

The answer again is a resounding yes. Again, at a system level the counterfactual is that we would be worse off without these relationships. In general, and as Bronfenbrenner's model of the ecology of human development so eloquently explained, the more that communities are connected with their schools, and in particular where there are shared practices and a two-way information flow, the better the developmental outcomes (Bronfenbrenner, 2009). This a very robust finding and holds across the range of valued outcomes for children, including their social and emotional development outcomes (Robinson et al., 2009; Sheridan et al., 2019).

But, clearly, having schools that relate to their communities is not sufficient to guarantee equitable outcomes. Other factors are at play. Just as in the case of the other strengths, we know a lot about how the relationships work and how to make them work. Sometimes they are present by default and little deliberate fostering is needed. This is the case when we talk about families having cultural capital for schools. The ways families with high cultural capital socialise their children match (are closely related to) school practices and the knowledge valued by schools. But we also know we can build the relationships so that the school and its local communities become closely connected and the power of the close relationships is harnessed.

For example, modelling high quality practices, such as frequent highly interactive reading to preschool children in early learning centres, is a very powerful mechanism to build the de facto relationship with parents and whānau. This was found when researchers in the Growing Up in New Zealand longitudinal study established that attending a teacher-led centre where these practices were in place increased the odds that families and whānau who were typically less likely to engage in these practices increased their use. The information flow between parents and whānau and the professional educators provided a mechanism for adding to practices (Thomas et al., 2019),

One of the relationships we have not been good at is the relationship between schools. This picture of being our "own worst enemy" was described in Chapter 4. The legacy of the Tomorrow's Schools policy was limited collaboration and co-operation between schools, and competition and inward-looking professional learning. We began the process of developing a sense of collective responsibility and sharing of effective practices between schools but as the most recent OECD commentary on our system notes, these relationships provide conditions for being better and there is still much more to do.[44]

The COVID experience taught us how important partnerships are. The finding that having partnerships with the local community organisations was critical to delivery of infrastructure and tools was one thing. But the rapid shift to online learning immediately threw into sharp relief the role of parents and whānau, and the teachers' role in being able to engage with them to give agency to the children and at the same time have appropriate guidance and support functions.

There is a major research agenda here. It is to understand how best for parents and whānau to engage with their children during online learning at home, or even post-COVID where there are forms of hybrid learning which involve more time online at home. This is under quite unfamiliar circumstances where they are not expected to become the teacher, and where children and adolescents are not engaged in homework in the usual sense, but rather doing their schoolwork at home.

What we do know is that some parents and whānau relished the engagement with their tamariki. Many were resilient and quite adaptive carrying out this role, sometimes in the face of considerable difficulty such as limitations in devices and the access available in the home, and balancing their own work needs (Hunia, et al., 2020).

---

[44] https://www.oecd-ilibrary.org/economics/
oecd-economic-surveys-new-zealand-2024_603809f2-en

Being creative

The last theme is a little different from the rest. Being creative is like being literate; it can be considered a "good" in and of itself. Nevertheless, the question can still be posed. Is having a system that is creative or that enables educators' creativity in any way useful to our twin goals of an educational system that is excellent and equitable?

If we consider the impact on students, the answer to that question is more straightforward. A number of recent analyses indicate important outcomes for students' wellbeing from deliberate acts of creativity in the classroom (O'Connor et al., 2020). Interventions that promote creativity have been used effectively after devastating events such as bushfires in Australia, earthquakes here in Aotearoa New Zealand, and for the COVID-19 pandemic recovery. These analyses suggest a causal path, which links the increased wellbeing with success in learning.

There is an answer that directs the question of the role of creativity to teaching. The answer in this case is that being creative, in the sense of local design and being enterprising and innovative, are features of teaching when conceived as a form of expertise. I have used this term in relationship to teaching several times already in this book. This is the key to the strength in our system, a particular form of expertise.

Our teachers need to have what has come to be called "adaptive expertise" (Darling-Hammond & Bransford, 2005). This carries connotations, like a jazz musician, of being able to do the basics but also being able to extemporise and move in and out of styles depending on interactions with others. An early use of the term "adaptive expertise" was in a book with elements of future forecasting, about what teaching in the 21st century should look like. In 2005, Linda Darling-Hammond and John Bransford, representing the National Academy of Education, drew a distinction between routine or technical experts (those experts who have developed a core set of competencies that they apply with greater and greater efficiency) and adaptive experts (those who continuously add to their knowledge and skills). These teachers change their core competencies and expand the breadth and depth of their expertise. It is this latter group of teachers who are seen as not just ideal but necessary for effective teaching now and in the future.

When we add content into this expertise, we need an additional concept of "design expertise" to capture the idea that teachers need to design the curriculum on the ground rather than follow simple prescriptions. Our teachers are expected to be able to design content integrating multiple domains of knowledge. The list includes the knowledge of an area of learning such as mathematics or science, the known progressions in this domain, and the typical tangles students get into in their learning. They need to know how to untangle these knots, armed with the varieties of instructional moves that can be made depending on the learner's current knowledge state and their needed knowledge state. This list is that part of the expertise that Lee Shulman called Pedagogical Content Knowledge (PCK), revisited and elaborated by Darling-Hammond and Bransford (2005).

To these we add the moment-by-moment decision making—the design of the activities that enact the curriculum and reflect the backgrounds and event knowledge of the current learners. We can add the capability to learn and modify and iterate through constant monitoring and feedback loops. The list goes on. It is why we should value teachers as extraordinary experts, and accord them the highest possible status, with terms and conditions that reflect their critical role.

If teachers are creative and can promote creativity with students, then this strength should contribute to the system's effectiveness, measured in wellbeing and in terms of learning in subject areas. Again, the answer is clearly not enough. If creativity contributes to wellbeing as the uses for trauma recovery suggest, then we are certainly not being creative enough. Our wellbeing data are not impressive. That is a cruel understatement. From the incidence of bullying through to feelings of alienation and on to the abysmal levels of anxiety and depression and suicide, we are among the worst in the OECD.

The answer to the question of why there is not more of a difference, repeated for each theme and present in the last theme of creativity, is both simple and at the same time complex. At a system level, being able to act consistently and with guaranteed skills is harder than the proverbial rocket science. We are not skilled at translating these grand themes into effective practices that are consistently applied nationally. They are strengths, present in pumped-up classrooms but weakly present in others. We don't apply the practices widely and deeply enough and at a national scale. We are too variable in our practices that embody these themes.

Four big challenges to being better

Capitalising on these strengths requires solving four big educational challenges identified in each of the chapters. The first is reducing the variability in what we do best, the corollary of which is being more consistent in being able to deliver each of the strengths. The second is being able to implement the strongest examples at scale (scalability). Building the capability at all levels of the system to engage with and apply the best of our practices is a third major challenge. The fourth is the sustainability of all of the above in the presence of change, as we adapt to changes in staff, students, communities, curriculum demands, system goals, and successive governments with different policy agendas.

Each of these is made even more challenging by shifting to teaching which can move between online and face-to-face, often within brief windows of time. Solving these challenges in the face of a complex, open, multilayered, and dynamic national system is a big ask. But if we are to do better for all our ākonga, communities, whānau, kaiako, and schools, these challenges must be solved. Our incapacity to act as well as we should is exacerbated by limited resources, starkly revealed in the picture for students with disabilities.

Take the challenge of variability. It is inherent in educational systems, at every level from granular to macro units of analysis (McNaughton, 2011). In Aotearoa New Zealand, variability in practices, and in the effects of teaching and learning outcomes, can be seen within classrooms and between classrooms, within schools and between schools, within and between clusters of schools, and across the regions. We need to embed all our strengths more consistently, at scale and with guaranteed capability, to be sustained.

These challenges are in essence the Achilles' heel of our strengths (Lai et al., 2020). The requirement to be local in the context of a great deal of school autonomy and relatively low prescription means all teachers need to be very good at what they do. There are weaknesses in our selection for teaching, in our initial teacher education, and in further professional development, to say nothing of the resourcing differences between schools in high-SES communities versus low-SES communities. The variability is such that we can't guarantee universally high-quality coverage. This variability magnifies inequalities.

For over a decade the go-to explanation at a system level for why we haven't solved our intractable equity problem and reversed the decline in excellence against international benchmarks has been the "quality of teaching" (Hattie, 2009). A number of high-level analyses created a tipping point for widespread adoption of this focus. These included the statistical process of parsing of variability in student achievement and the ranking of effect sizes of different influences on achievement through meta-analyses. The conclusion was that the greatest effects are with the teacher's instruction. Other sources of variance—such as students' language, culture, and identity, and socialisation practices at home—although significant, were seen as sources the system couldn't focus on for change. Or, looking at variability in outcomes such as achievement *within* schools as being greater than the variability *between* schools, leading to the conclusion the SES and other differences between schools are not as influential as what teachers do within a school (Alton-Lee, 2003).

Both are oversimplifications and can lead to the wrong conclusions being drawn. For example, the relationship between home and school that can build co-ordinated practices is certainly something in which schools have a role. Understanding and building on the resources a child brings to school is, in fact, the essence of excellent teaching, as our child-centred approach has demonstrated. Actually, while the average difference between schools is not as great as the within-school variability, the variability in achievement between the lowest

SES schools (what was decile 1) and the highest (what was decile 10) on average is as great as the average variability within schools in achievement. It matters greatly which schools our children attend. Sadly, on average, the student outcomes and the resources in a decile 1 school are markedly different from those in a decile 10 school. A simple way to show this is to look at the sports equipment, the music equipment, the places that student groups go for educational trips, and all the "discretionary" spending available in each set of schools. It is a sobering look (Wylie, 2012).

The decile system was designed to overcome the "on average" differences between schools but it has proven to be a blunt instrument. There is now a more precise tool, the equity index, to better target the funding (Ministry of Education, 2019b), which is being evaluated for its effectiveness as a targeting mechanism to overcome disparities. But the measure of effectiveness of the new mechanism will not be whether it better targets the funding, but whether it targets with sufficient funding spent on the resources to make a real difference to those who need it.

The latter question depends in turn on how much we know about the costs of making a difference. For example, what does it take to make up differences in achievement in curriculum level terms apparent (on average again) in the cohorts arriving at decile 1 schools, in order to accelerate their rate of progress to match national expectations in the benchmark levels for leaving school, such as NCEA Level 2? Having said this, it is important to reiterate that there are decile 1 schools in which children make year-on-year progress that is greater than some decile 10 schools. And this points to the central claim of this book, that we have strengths and that we can make a difference with these strengths but there are challenges to doing this across the system. Let's solve the problematic variability.

The focus on teaching quality led to a focus on identifying better and better instructional procedures for teachers via initial teacher education and ongoing professional learning and development.[45]

---

45 For commentary on the meta-analyses and variability issue, see McNaughton (2011). For variablity within and between schools, see Schmidt et al. (2015).

This is a question of making sure instructional capability is high. But that focus on quality misses the bigger challenges. These are what conditions enable the most effective instruction to be implemented consistently at scale, and able to be taken to scale with adaptation and to meet local conditions. In order to do that we need to think more widely than just instructional techniques.

The bases for guaranteeing greater consistency in use of effective teaching include the need to rethink initial and ongoing teacher education. One reason for needing to consider these conditions is the tension between generalist and specialist teaching in primary schools. In primary schooling, we expect our teachers to be generalists in eight learning areas, ranging from English and literacy through science to PE and health. In addition, we require them to be able to promote the social and emotional skills that we call the key competencies. These are the valued social and emotional skills, such as self-regulation (called *managing self* in the English curriculum document) and skills of collaboration (called *getting on with others*). This is a portfolio of skills and knowledge that is truly awesome in scope.

Primary teachers, most of whom have a first degree in teaching or education, typically do not have a specialist qualification in any one or other of the subject areas. This is very noticeable in science and maths.[46] Fewer than 5% of our teachers at Year 4 and fewer than 20% at Year 8 have a science major or advanced or additional science training or qualifications. Just 14% or our Year 5 students have a teacher with any sort of specialist qualification in maths, compared with nearly 50% across a range of other countries. Our teachers face a daunting task, relying on one or two content courses in their teaching degree and professional development.

Our teachers have been very clear about their needs. Many enjoy teaching maths and science. But a fifth of Year 5 teachers have low confidence in teaching maths and many don't rate what professional development they access very highly. It is no wonder that we have

---

46 A summary is contained in the report by The Royal Society Te Apārangi Expert Advisory Panel (2021). See also https://www.educationcounts.govt.nz/__data/assets/pdf_file/0007/192913/NMSSA-2017-Science.pdf and Rendall et al. (2020).

variability and don't have the capability. However, the same teachers may have generically good pedagogical or instructional skills which may be able to be applied in some areas such as teaching reading and writing, and teaching PE and health. In secondary schooling we may have the opposite problem. It's having variable pedagogical expertise of the sort that their primary colleagues have, to enact a local curriculum and establish powerful relationships.

To make matters worse, there are additional drivers of variability in expertise, exaggerated by our self-managing schools design (Wylie, 2012). Resources that make a difference are not equally distributed across schools and regions. All schools are not created equal. This can be seen in who gets access to highly qualified specialist subject teachers, both in the primary and secondary sectors. It can be seen in infrastructure, in the curriculum-related resources such as digital devices or musical and sports equipment. It can be seen in the widely variable amount of non-government funding schools have access to, raised by the school's community to access extra resources and extra curricula experiences. Without equitable resourcing across schools, communities, districts, and regions we will continue to have inequitable distributions of the needed capability of our teachers.

The focus on quality teaching has meant that we haven't focused as much as we should have on what is a much more complex problem for educational sciences. This is, the problem that has been posed as "What works for whom, under what conditions at scale, and over time?" (Bryk et al., 2015). This science goes by names such as implementation science, improvement science, or performance science. It needs to solve why it is difficult to take the strengths that are not widespread to scale, in ways that guarantee consistent expertise which is sustainable.

So how do we change?

Knowing the problem is not hard. The hard part is solving the problem. There are seven changes we could make to capitalise on the strengths, building the needed capability nationally in a system which is consistently excellent and equitable, and where effective practices are continuously improved and sustainable.

- Raising the status of teaching, including but not only through terms and conditions and pay.
- Rapid expansion of Māori medium and a Māori teaching workforce, together with a rapid expansion of a Pasifika teaching workforce.
- Increasing the clarity and detail of how to design a local curriculum.
- Being child-centred: critical literacy and collaborative reasoning.
- A life-course approach to change.
- Using readily available levers to reduce the variability in and capability for high-quality practices in schools.
- Fast development of AI and ML powered tools for everyone's wellbeing.

1. Raising the status of teaching

In the first chapter I recounted my conversation with a Minister who asked me to identify the 10 things I thought we should do to make substantial change. My list ended up only five items long because several of those on a longer list were components of a general focus of *raising the status of teaching*.

The status of teaching is a problem in Aotearoa New Zealand, where fewer than half (46%) of our Year 7 to Year 10 teachers think that the teaching profession is valued, which contrasts with six to seven out of 10 teachers saying they are valued in Singapore and Finland.[47] An unpublished 2010 survey (for TeachNZ) of prospective teacher education applicants in Auckland with a first degree indicated that teaching was seen as a "Plan B"—meaning, if I don't get into what I want to get into at university I will go teaching. Status seems to matter, as shown by relationships with student achievement across countries (Schleicher, 2018). The caveat is that we don't have analyses that reliably show causality as distinct from a correlation, and it is only one of several contributing factors to a more consistently equitable and excellent system.

---

47 https://www.educationcounts.govt.nz/__data/assets/pdf_file/0013/170212/TALIS-Insights-teacher-self-efficacy-and-job-satisfaction.docx.pdf

While some lessons can be learned from other jurisdictions, history, cultural, and societal contexts play a very significant role in determining the specific conditions associated with and needed for increasing status (see Robinson et al., 2011). But common themes do emerge in comparisons of high performing and impressively improving jurisdictions (Auguste et al., 2010; Darling-Hammond, 2013; Mourshed et al., 2010). They attract the top graduates from high schools (from the top third in Singapore), often providing financial support in the form of a salary or stipend during training, and commitments on both sides to employment after training. Several have required, or are shifting fully towards, a Master's level qualification.

The COVID conditions have had an impact on the attractiveness if not the status of teaching. As with the Global Financial Crisis, applications for enrolment went up substantially in the first year of COVID. They remained high in postgraduate enrolments 2 years into the pandemic, but have dropped back to pre-pandemic levels for undergraduate teacher education, and are dropping at several universities. Without good evidence it is hard to know what to make of the pattern. But in Auckland the drop at the undergraduate and diploma levels has been attributed by teacher educators and by schools to the impact of repeated lockdowns on family/whānau, hardship, and disengagement from school at Year 13 for a variety of reasons, not the least of which is needing employment income for families.

Raising status involves addressing several areas.[48]

Selection and qualifications

Raising status is about making the role highly desirable, highly regarded, and highly selective. Teachers' pay that recognises the highly skilled expert nature of teaching and the direct impact on individual, community, and national outcomes—including productivity—matters. The example from Finland, where teachers have very high status, is of having somewhat higher pay at both primary and secondary levels

---

48 The recent OECD commentary on the education system sees this as a priority and provides further evidence of the needed areas of change and the evidence for impacts https://www.oecd-ilibrary.org/economics/oecd-economic-surveys-new-zealand-2024_603809f2-en

than the OECD average, but not exorbitantly higher (OECD, 2022). They certainly are not an outlier on salary scales.

Raising the status draws on a number of interdependent components, one of which is the type and level of qualification that teachers have. Subject-related degrees and knowledge through higher qualifications can be related to pedagogical quality and instructional effectiveness (Manning et al., 2019).[49] But there are three parts to the evidence. One is the level of qualification. As the Finnish example of requiring a Master's level qualification suggests, recognising the need for a postgraduate-level qualification to enter the profession is associated with higher standing. Attracting highly talented people into teaching would be aided by setting a higher benchmark for qualifications, especially for primary teachers. The second is what is addressed as the next component—it is the skills and knowledge developed through the qualification. The third is the level of knowledge and skills attained in the academic domains and the extent of Pedagogical Content Knowledge (PCK). This need for more specific knowledge and skills within the higher-level qualification is discussed next too.

A research and evidence orientation

The Finnish practice is to require primary and secondary teachers to have a Master's degree with a research thesis. Our initial teacher education should require a research-based Master's for all levels, from teacher-led early learning services through to secondary. The research experience is the part where teachers learn to understand a field, test ideas, use evidence, and engage in the continuous improvement needed for the adaptive and design expertise. It is one basis for the PCK and design and problem-solving skills I identified earlier. It adds to the capability within schools to act on the evidence and engage in design and redesign cycles to better meet aims.

We celebrate inquiry through the curriculum and in most forms of professional development. However, what we have been reviewing is capability in addition to inquiry. Presently, as described in curriculum resources and as practised, inquiry is the stock-in-trade of informal

---

49   See also https://www.oecd-ilibrary.org/economics/
     oecd-economic-surveys-new-zealand-2024_603809f2-en

and formal assessment. It is part of business as usual, contributing to the dynamic day-to-day adaptive expertise. It is not what is required in a research thesis. Inquiry as it stands today runs the risk of being superficial and performative if seen as a proxy for the research skills and knowledge our teachers need.

Specialist teaching

Teacher status is related to working conditions including promotional pathways and recognised specialisms. A crucial step to take in this regard would be to have specialist teaching in core learning areas in primary schools: in Years 1–3 to promote foundational skills and knowledge, and from Year 3 or Year 4 onwards in core curriculum areas. We have low levels of achievement in science and mathematics from Year 4 to Year 8. The low confidence in teaching maths and science from Years 4 to 8 is associated with this. So too are low levels of advanced qualifications in these areas. There are other reasons for doing this. Generalist teaching requires lesson preparation time, assessing, and marking across all the eight learning areas. This is a source of stress. The more compliance associated with marking and teacher preparation, the more stress. Over a quarter of our teachers (Year 7–10) report experiencing "a lot" of occupational stress (see OECD, 2019; Sims, 2021; and Talis, 2018).[50]

Secondary schools are, by definition, discipline or subject-area based. But in parallel with the argument for primary teaching, teachers are required to be many things to many students and colleagues, including acting de facto as counsellors, providing life guidance, and being physical and mental health paraprofessionals. Specialists for these needs of adolescents already exist but the coverage is limited and variable. Our evidence is that the more school-based health services in a school, the better students' mental health (Denny et al., 2018). More of these specialists at secondary school are needed in pressing areas of social and emotional learning and wellbeing.

Our evidence also shows, however, that to enable transfer and robust learning, subject teachers need to be able use their subject

---

50   Further evidence of levels of confidence and stress is here: https://www.oecd-ilibrary.org/economics/oecd-economic-surveys-new-zealand-2024_603809f2-en

areas to promote what we currently call the key competencies. When these are considered from the point of view of social and emotional skills such as self-regulation, and social skills requiring empathy and perspective taking, it is clear that these need to be part of everyday teaching in subject areas. It is clearer perhaps in subject English or te reo Māori and in literacy, where forms of empathy and perspective-taking can be developed through fiction reading, critical literacy, and communication; but it is present in collaborative reasoning in science or in critical investigation in local history, too. We will need to reduce compliance costs associated with assessment and accountability, and other workload pressures in order to increase the specialist focus with greater attention to the key competencies. The Years 7–10 teachers I referred to earlier also estimate that time spent on actual teaching in a week was less than half their overall hours and below the OECD average.

Specialist support is one of several urgent system improvements needed for neurodivergent students. The urgent needs echo the other themes of knowing and responding to each child's needs (not rigid programmes), partnerships, and localised collectives of resourcing (Hood & Hume, 2024).

Supported pathways

Yet another component of status is the conditions associated with training, especially of being supported in the preparatory years and into the beginning teacher role. Singapore, as noted earlier, takes the academically highest achieving graduates. We need to attract similarly talented graduates from secondary schools and, as argued above, require high level tertiary qualifications which include subject specialty pathways for primary as well as secondary teachers.

We need more Māori and Pasifika teachers. Being better at being child-centred and designing local curricula for Māori and Pasifika children is greatly aided by the match between the teacher's cultural competence, language skills, and identity and those of the student. The evidence for this relationship for students traditionally not well-served by schools—the children from marginalised communities—is very clear now and the processes through which it enhances learning are well known (for international reviews, see Darling-Hammond et al., 2020; Redding, 2019).

Unfortunately, if we were to select only from the top third of graduates from secondary schools we would limit the pathways to becoming teachers for Māori and Pasifika students and those from communities facing material hardships. If we were to require a first degree as entry to all teacher education levels we would add further to systemic inequalities. In order to also increase the number of Māori and Pasifika teachers we need extensive scholarship, studentship, and internship systems that identify and support prospective trainees from secondary schools, and add through these mechanisms funds to reduce the financial burden of advanced study on families and whānau.

Solving complex pressing social problems requires thinking in terms of the life-course, an approach which is proposed in a number of areas by science advisors in the social sector (Gluckman, 2017; McNaughton, 2020; Gerrard, 2018).[51] We need an intergenerational strategy to build the Māori and Pacific workforce, with a long-term commitment to supported pathways from secondary schooling into and through a first degrees and beyond.

Systematic collaboration

Some of the relationships that have been undermined are those between teachers across classrooms within a school and those between teachers across schools. Teachers have tended to be in relatively independent classrooms, and schools have tended to function as relatively autonomous units. That is not say that professional groupings have not existed. The subject professional groupings, for example, have been strong.

But the deliberate and direct sharing of effective practices has been ad hoc and designed to get over the autonomy at a class and at a school level. The sharing and interrogation of practices, which reflects the innovative and adaptive design work of teachers in situ, is

---

[51] These reports are available on The Prime Ministers' Chief Science Advisor's website: https://www.pmcsa.ac.nz

becoming more regular. The rolling back of autonomous units created by Tomorrow's Schools provides a platform for this.

This is definitely something at which we could be better. The evidence for why comes from several sources (e g. Fullan et al., 2015; Hattie, 2015; Schleicher, 2018.). One is the meaning-making capability we have already noted, including the effects of specific types of collective analysis such as "lesson study". Another draws on decades of research on the effects of both individual and collective forms of efficacy (knowing about and having feelings of being in control) on performance. This has been relabelled recently as Collective Teacher Efficacy (CTE), the school community's shared beliefs in collective capability to bring about the activities needed to meet achievement goals. It is among the most significant determinants of schools' impact on achievement.

2. Rapid expansion of Māori medium and Māori and Pasifika teaching workforce

We know that a major enabler of Māori achievement is living in a whānau with strong Māori identity, language, and culture. Attending Māori-medium schools increases the odds of achievement even more. To add to these, a major impact on achievement is having teachers who are Māori or who are very familiar with mātauranga Māori and te ao Māori, and this can be shown in English-medium secondary schools. Rapidly expanding high quality Māori-medium education and the roles and leadership of Māori teachers across the whole system would build on the strengths of being child-centred, leveraging off the local curriculum, and trying to be bicultural.

This is not an easy task. I argued earlier for pipeline growth of Māori teachers, and this is especially pressing for Māori medium. It can't be done without other changes in place. One is increasing the status of teaching, which requires much wider and more realistic systems of scholarships, studentships, and internships, targeted for Māori and Pasifika students and those from low income and high unemployment communities. There are issues of infrastructure and resourcing, as practical as buildings, but including the curriculum tools identified in other changes, such as assessments that are designed by and for Māori medium.

All of these pieces need to be in place if we are to change our (in)equitable educational profile for Māori and Pasifika. Importantly, the changes to be made have an evidence base, as well as being Treaty-led and ethically justified. The central problems in the system I have identified, however, apply as much to this need as to the others. It is making sure that there is consistent high effectiveness as teachers, with guaranteed high-quality resourcing across all local sites.

3. Increasing the clarity and detail of being local

The local curriculum strength is driven in part by the very limited prescription in curricula and syllabi. There are, of course, resources around the curriculum and pedagogy, but as we have noted the onus is on the teacher to do the hard work of making the curriculum locally relevant.

There have been arguments over many years that we should add more clarity and detail from the centre, and I agree (Tomorrow's Schools Independent Taskforce, 2018; Wylie, 2012). This is consistent with the general push to raise the status in line with the complexities and responsibilities of the role. It is being clearer about what our children and young people need to know and be able to do and adding that detail into the curriculum with appropriate resources. The risk, however, is that we could tip the balance towards technical expertise. It could imperil the adaptive and design expertise needed to create the local curriculum.

This process has begun with a refresh of the curriculum and the development of a Common Practice Model for literacy and maths. It has meant, as I noted earlier, academic historians laying out what content and understanding is needed for the study of history in Aotearoa. There is now a solid framework on which to build the local curriculum in this area. It is captured in three big ideas (Māori history is foundational; colonisation and its consequences have been central; our history has been shaped by the exercise and effects of power), three national contexts (social linkages; those with natural resources; and those of authority, power, and control associated with the Te Tiriti o Waitangi | Treaty of Waitangi), and three inquiry practices (identifying and using sequences; identifying and critiquing sources; interpreting the past).[52]

To make this come alive in each local context will require extensive resourcing. This too has already begun. One of the examples the then Minister of Education used to launch the consultation on the recommended curriculum bears directly on the local curriculum question. "In Te Tai Tokerau, for example, I know people will be interested in learning about the battle that took place in Ruapekapeka during the Northern Wars in the 1800s," Minister Hipkins said (Cooke, 2021). The local battle is used as a context for the big ideas, contexts, and inquiry processes. Students and teachers in other areas where the land wars occurred can do likewise, in all cases using the local events as the key to unlocking the curriculum themes. For example, the Minister went on to say, "In Waikato, ākonga may learn about the invasion of Waikato led by Governor George Grey and the implications this had for people living in the region."

How does this deal to the equity challenge? The local curriculum has always been one of the routes we could have taken more deliberately and with greater consistency to solve this. Being local and being child-centred require connecting with each child, their event knowledge and their identity, culture, and language. In literacy, we have used the metaphor of window and mirror texts to illustrate the point and the linkages with the curriculum. Seeing oneself and one's cultural resources clearly reflected in texts is one half of the equation. But once again, it is not that this is a revelation or that we don't do this already. The core issue is captured in the concepts above of deliberation and consistency. The challenge is how to reduce the variability, building the capability to do this more generally at scale and in a sustained way.

---

52 https://aotearoahistories.education.govt.nz/

4. Being child-centred: Critical literacy and collaborative reasoning

There is a pressing need our children face, the solution to which could build on our strengths in being child-centred, creative, and solution-oriented. It is to solve a stark problem which existed before digital tools and social media, but is now of even greater significance because of them.

Access to social media and other digital platforms increases the risks of exposure to and use of misinformation. Our students are threatened through greater access to and amplification of various distortions of information, untruths, stereotypes, conspiracy theories, harassment, bullying, and prejudice. The platforms have affordances that increase the threat. But they also provide a means to not only counteract the threat but also proactively enable students to be resilient, well informed, critically engaged, and, as a group, inclusive and supportive of each other. Catalytic events such as the Christchurch terror attack and COVID-19 pandemic show just how urgent it is that we plan for and build resilience.

Critical literacy, which goes by a variety of terms—some of which are descriptive ("media and information literacy") and some more abstract ("epistemic vigilance")—is increasingly recognised as important for resilience in the face of these threats, and to build an informed citizenry. Critical literacy is a focus in many educational systems, but across most we haven't worked out how to educate for advanced forms, where students reason effectively; navigate sources of information confidently; judge and critique the accuracy, credibility, reliability, and believability of online information; and understand bias and perspective (Fraillon et al., 2018; McGrew et al., 2017).

Perhaps the one exception brings us back to the catalyst for writing this book. It is the often and widely admired case of Finland, which in 2014 started an anti fake news campaign. It is comprehensive and meant to prepare all citizens for threats in the complex digital world, with a particular focus on being able to identify and counter false information designed to undermine the country's politics. The centrepiece is a 2016 revision to the critical thinking curriculum from kindergarten to 12 years, foregrounding identifying misinformation. The President is quoted as saying: "The first line of defence is the kindergarten teacher."[53] I agree.

The generally low levels internationally of this form of critical literacy raise the question of how best to prepare students. In general, there are two complementary components. There is a community of practice component and there is a deliberate teaching component. Effective communities of the classroom and of the school feature caring teacher and student relationships, clear norms, expectations, and practices to create conditions for the acquisition of the specific skills (Abrami et al., 2015; Reznitskaya et al., 2009). Experimental demonstrations show face-to-face communities of practice can be built in classrooms, which develop the criticality and reasoning skills including those that are *inter*personal (e.g., sociability, perspective taking), and those that are *intra*personal skills (e.g., self-regulation) necessary to engage effectively in the practices of the community. There is as yet limited evidence for how best to do this in online communities (Mair, et al., 2019; McNaughton et al., 2019; Reznitskaya et al., 2009).

Different approaches have been used for promoting the specific skills. There is limited systematic research evidence for the most effective approaches that guarantee transfer from classroom to everyday use with information sources. Currently, the consensus is that a mixed approach, involving explicit instruction in thinking critically embedded in major subjects coupled with some dedicated coursework focused on the critical literacy (media literacy) skills—such as in civics or philosophy courses—likely works best for transfer, as a study of Finnish schools compared with US schools suggests (Horn & Veermans, 2019).

The evidence for our students in Aotearoa New Zealand is mixed. There is a focus on critical literacy in subject English classes at secondary level, with up to 80% of students reporting learning about the consequences of making information public online; judging whether to

---

53 https://www.nordicpolicycentre.org.au/media_literacy_education_in_finland

trust information from the internet; or comparing different webpages and deciding the relevance of information. On the PISA reading literacy assessment (OECD, 2018), our 15-year-olds performed significantly higher than the average across 77 countries, and similar to Poland, Australia, the United States, the United Kingdom, Japan, Denmark, and Sweden.[54] Finland was one of the top countries, which is consistent with their more comprehensive approach, and our students scored significantly lower than those in Finland.

The contrasting picture, however, is that almost one-fifth (19%) of students on the PISA reading literacy were below the OECD basic proficiency level, and there are large gender (girls outperform boys), ethnicity, and SES differences. In English classrooms, Māori and Pasifika students and students from low-decile schools tend to receive instruction that is less challenging, with less of a focus on these more complex aspects of literacy, and there are markedly lower participation rates in complex English standards for Level 2 NCEA (30–40% lower). There is also evidence of a low focus on critical literacy teaching in low-decile primary schools (Wilson et al., 2016; Jesson et al., 2018; McNaughton et al., 2019).

In Aotearoa New Zealand, the curriculum vision statement refers to developing critical and creative thinkers, and in each learning area there is reference to students being critical. However, the refresh will need to elaborate what these critical literacy skills are and how best to teach them.

5. A life-course approach to change

A life-course approach to system change is needed. Again, this is related to the issues of variability and building capability. Inoculation or single component explanations for why we aren't as equitable or excellent as we should be are no longer adequate, if they ever were. Take reading achievement, for example. It is at best incomplete to pose the achievement problem at 15 years as due to only one of the following: a lack of reading to preschoolers; limited systematic phonics

---

[54] https://www.educationcounts.govt.nz/publications/series/PISA/pisa-2018/reading-literacy-achievement-senior-secondary-school

instruction; variable "third tier" interventions in Years 1–3; low expectations; the need for redesigned strategy instruction; more subject literacy teaching; overcoming digital distractions; too few "mirror" texts; disengagement and wellbeing needs; lack of specialist teaching; downward pressure of NCEA, etc.

Each of these components is important. Each of these is, to a greater or lesser degree, important for the life course of a student to 15 years. But they are not by themselves sufficient to guarantee high achievement and reduced inequalities and, more importantly, each has a contingent importance. That is, each depends on other conditions being in place for maximum and long-term effect. But fixing one part of a complex dynamic trajectory of development relies for its longer-term effectiveness on fixing the other connected parts. We need to go beyond thinking that if we just got early childhood right, or if we solved the issues in secondary, that would be enough. It is not a zero-sum game, in which we do more of one thing, but then do less of or don't do the other things that are needed.

Rather, all the pieces must be working well if we are to build a more equitable and excellent system. A better system will result from optimising learning and development across all ages, and consequently identifying how to be better across the life course, during sensitive periods and across transitions. We need to urgently address the system needs at these points.

Enabling greater coherence across early learning and schooling will take some concerted effort. Early learning is a case in point. An open market has exaggerated variability in guidance and developmental supports. An outmoded and not fit-for-purpose prevailing ideology has used the taonga of the early childhood curriculum *Te Whāriki* to celebrate individual pathways of development but resist monitoring children's development in ways that would enable judgements about quality and improvement.

The net effect has been at best to have no impact on poverty and resource-driven inequities, which are palpable on entry to school. At worst, given what we know about Matthew effects (rich get richer) and the need for targeted guidance, their effects are likely to have been exaggerated overall. Greater capability to understand specific aspects of development over the preschool years as they provide building blocks for ongoing learning at school is needed, which is dependent on advances in assessment and monitoring tools and evidence-based designs for guidance.

There are barriers to sharing valuable information about children. An absence of systematic and usable descriptions of a child's development, coupled with confidentiality requirements, means information is difficult to share with the primary school. In this first and each of the following transitions, variability in systematically linked records of progress and achievement and other more qualitative data undermines being able to manage and respond to needs.

To make matters more complicated, there is variable early childhood provision for the transition to school, reflecting the existence of the competitive open market for services and a variety of types of provision for early learning services. Not all the children from the geographically local early childhood sites will go to the local primary school. The corollary is that not all children going to a school are local. To a degree, different types of early childhood provision are competitive, through differences in overarching educational philosophy and because of a mix of state-funded and private for-profit and not-for-profit sites. This makes it difficult for a primary school to partner with a particular local early childhood provider to systematically prepare and activate a pathway for all children.

6. *Using readily available levers: Specificity, evidence, and accountability*

In a radio interview on 1 February 2021 discussing maths achievement, Iona Holsted, the Secretary of Education, identified a central dilemma. She referred to the conundrum the system has of the balance between loose and tight: how much specification is needed for everything from curricula to pedagogy. What is the role of the centre in leading and defining curricula and pedagogy versus the role of the local, schools in their local context? How tight should the specifications be? How much looseness should there be to enable the agency entailed in being local?

It is a complex balancing act. But the weight of evidence, such as the evidence about science and maths teaching in the middle primary school years, or the evidence for how teachers need to be able to construct a local curriculum for history, is that we have been too loose. To continue the use of the mechanical analogy, we are now changing the balance by using levers we haven't fully used before that could make a difference to our excellence and equity aims. These levers include greater specification in the curriculum about what our children should know and be able to do in the major learning areas at critical junctures across schooling. If enacted well, this will increase the collective wisdom and understanding of expected progressions and reduce variable interpretations of the curriculum. There are other levers I have noted in the previous chapters. The specifications for teachers' practising certificates, for example, if enacted well, will contribute to reducing the variability in being bicultural.

Other levers we could pull more firmly include the centre's data curation and dissemination functions, providing all schools with timely and fit-for-purpose data ranging from achievement patterns to wellbeing and social cohesion outcomes. With added interpretations and commentary using evidence-based insights, usable and valuable feedback loops would provide the means for continuous improvement at the school level. While not the only necessary component of effective school change (leadership is another), having an evidence base for redesigning what one does is critical.

Our research team at Waipapa Taumata Rau University of Auckland has spent a decade identifying and demonstrating the significance of this capability at a school and cluster level (Lai et al., 2020). The Washington State Institute for Public Policy evaluated interventions to build this capability as very cost effective and robust.[55] Having the digital online infrastructure and evidence-based "meaning-making" at

---

55 http://www.wsipp.wa.gov/BenefitCost?topicId=4

scale, as part of the centre's capability, would contribute to the reduction in variability.

I haven't said we need to use levers associated with accountability, such as performance-based pay. Overall there is little evidence for impacts on system-level performance, although it depends on how high teachers' salaries are in the jurisdictions where such accountability processes are used. Positive effects on system achievement levels are associated with low salary paying countries and negative effects with high salary paying countries.[56] Professional forms of accountability matter more across many jurisdictions. I also haven't said that a lever we could pull is to reinstate some form of standards-based external accountability system. The perverse outcomes of this are well known and we have recently experienced these (McNaughton, 2018).

7. Fast development of AI and ML powered tools for everyone's wellbeing

What if we could reduce the opportunity and compliance costs associated with formal assessments and the more mundane procedural aspects of teaching? The extensive formal assessment teachers carry out has two flow-on effects. One is that the time taken leads to a commensurate reduction in time to engage with students in ways that capitalise on our strengths. A recent estimate is that 20 to 40% of hours of teacher time could be saved with artificial intelligence (AI) and machine learning (ML) enabled tools (Bryant et al., 2020). Current evidence is that effective teachers use the time freed up just from students using devices in digitally enabled classrooms, to personalise learning and have creative, child-centred exchanges that extend and elaborate content.

It is early days, but the findings parallel those in the health sector (OECD, 2020). Very smart AI tools are already creating more efficient and accurate forms of diagnosis, and higher quality and more reliable surgery. AI may not replace the surgeon and the general practitioner; rather, it is likely to free them up to concentrate on the other aspects

---

56 For international evidence, see https://www.oecd.org/pisa/pisaproducts/pisainfocus/50328990.pdf. For local discussion, see Robinson et al. (2011).

of their work, particularly to do with the patient–doctor relationship and making personalised decisions about patient health and wellbeing. Under current conditions in classrooms it is very difficult to have extended time with students. One of the hardest asks of teachers, identified in the professional development literature, is to have complex personalised and extended content-rich exchanges with students.

The second negative outcome of compliance and opportunity cost is closely related to the need to spend more time in close pedagogical relationships in the classrooms. It is the impact on teachers' wellbeing that comes from time pressure and high workloads, and the sense of frustration at not having the time to engage effectively with learners (Schleicher, 2018). These developments could be considered "low-hanging fruit". It wouldn't take much to put in place the research and development programme that would deliver these assessments to schools. But there are more challenging tasks. These are the digital tools to increase valued aspects of the curriculum. This is not just the areas of knowledge, represented by smart tutoring tools.[57] These are still relatively low hanging and there are systems already for tutoring in English language, for example, or mathematics.

More challenging are the digital tools to impact on social and emotional skills. Despite being child-centred we are not sufficiently capable of supporting children to have reduced the appalling patterns of bullying and lowered wellbeing as one moves through the system, of anxiety and depression, and of suicide. However, there are developments in this area. Tools can be developed which increase the desperately needed skills of self-regulation, sociability, and empathy. This time it's not Finland we turn to but India, and increasingly our own nascent developments. In India the UNESCO Mahatma Gandhi Institute of Education for Peace and Sustainable Development (MGIEP) focuses on achieving the UN Sustainable Development Goal 4.7 towards education for building peaceful and sustainable societies across the world by developing programmes that promote social and emotional learning, innovate digital pedagogies, and empower the youth.[58] One of their

---

57   Just one example from China is squirrel technology: http://squirrelai.com/
58   https://mgiep.unesco.org/

research and development programmes involves the use of games for teaching social and emotional learning skills.

Being better through COVID

Our records show that very early on in the first series of lockdowns the Ministry of Education realised that this was a make-or-break time for students, for their wellbeing as much as for their learning. The Secretary of Education faced a national audience and said the pandemic had exposed disparities—there was a major equity issue to be solved. The issue was equitable access to and use of digital media.

From the viewpoint of children in lockdown, learning opportunities for curriculum coverage and core aspects of wellbeing such as anxiety or feeling in control and succeeding were compromised without connectivity, let alone an appropriate device (Dowden, 2022; ERO, 2021; Hunia et al., 2020; Meissel et al, 2021; Walker et al., 2021; Webber, 2021; Wenmouth, 2021). At the point of the first lockdown, it was estimated that approximately one-sixth of the country's 816,600 school students didn't have broadband at home, and were presumed not to have suitable devices either. Māori and Pasifika children and children from low-SES communities were over-represented, and the impact was exacerbated for those with multiple stresses such as unemployment and housing difficulties.

Early on there was evidence that students in the upper levels of secondary schooling facing the NCEA exams were most vulnerable. Their needs drove a focus on getting the connectivity and devices to them as a priority. The rapid response, warts and all, looked better than some other countries. Not good enough, though—halfway through the lockdown period a survey by Ngāti Whātua Ōrākei showed more than half of their NCEA-level students could only use their phones to try to do complex mathematics, and to write in-depth essays in te reo Māori or English.

Various solutions were mobilised, not always successfully. The mobilisation exposed a number of flaws as basic as not having a robust, up-to-date and accurate database held centrally that would enable modems and devices to be sent in a rapid response to where they were needed. Several "Plan Bs" were implemented. Hard packs of materials were delivered. There were dedicated Māori and parallel English-medium daily TV programmes. It is fair to say that the Ministry of Education acted very quickly. Despite not always getting it right, by June 2021 over 44,000 households had been connected to the internet for over 80,000 students, with over 34,000 devices delivered—70% of the laptops going to Years 10 to 13 students.

The evidence has yet to be fully analysed about how successful these responses were, judged in terms of both learning and wellbeing. The initial results for learning after the first set of lockdowns showed that achievement in reading and maths had not been impacted (unlike other jurisdictions), but there was evidence for an impact on writing. For wellbeing, like the international data, the picture is not simple. Some children, their whānau, and households showed considerable resilience, and many reported improved wellbeing and enjoyment of family and whānau time. But on the initial evidence, like the national response to the pandemic itself, we can certainly claim to be more successful than some others. One of the first inter-country surveys by the OECD estimated that about half of the students across 59 countries were able to access all or most of the curriculum (Reimers & Schleicher, 2020). New Zealand was considered well prepared, in terms of teacher knowledge and infrastructure. That preparedness, together with what I have claimed are our core strengths, may turn out to be an important lesson.

Final comments

One of the strengths on which I have focused is trying to be bicultural and how our system could use the strengths at hand to make a greater difference for ākonga Māori and their whānau. Other strengths apply also to how we could better meet our commitments to Pasifika learners and their communities, as well as those from communities with few material resources. Being child-centred, treating the local context and communities as resourceful for teaching and learning (rather than disadvantaged), engaging in mutually supportive relationships with communities, and using design expertise to support creativity and innovation are generalisable strengths. They are generalisable to these communities and those with students with disabilities. Being bicultural additionally serves as a basis for what we need to be able to achieve with these communities.

Lastly, there is comment to be made about recognising the role of research, evidence, and educational science in what we know and about what we could do in the wider Research, Science, and Innovation (RSI) landscape. Unlike health research, specific funding and priorities for educational research have not figured directly in pre-COVID statements about the RSI landscape by the Ministry of Business, Innovation and Employment (for example, Ministry of Business, Innovation and Employment, 2018). When funding for education is mentioned, it is in relationship to the general funding of universities via the mechanism of the Performance-Based Research Fund I described earlier.

But this is not direct funding available for educational research. All possible sources of funding—for research, research and development, and evaluation, through dedicated competitive funding as well as budget allocated within agencies—is likely less than $40m per year. The most prestigious competitive funding is the Teaching and Learning Research Initiative (TLRI) funding administered by the New Zealand Council for Educational Research, which allocates only $1.5m per year. By comparison, there is over $360m available for research and development in health (MBIE, 2018).

The value of education can be established in terms of personal benefits over a lifetime, collective benefits (e.g., to families, communities, and such), and national benefits (e.g., in terms of income or contributions to GDP). Just considering the contribution to GDP alone, at the time of writing Aotearoa New Zealand spends 1.3% of GDP on all research and development, but aspires to 2.0% and the OECD average is 2.4%. Considering not just research and development but also evaluation, in education it is around 0.3% of the total Vote Education spend.

The point is that if we want to do all of the above, we need a very robust and well-funded research and development and innovation capability. At the moment that capability is severely limited.

Despite this, there is a growing realisation that solving our excellence and equity issues will require much more systematic funding of educational sciences. Noting the inequalities starkly exposed through the lockdowns and with the shift to online learning and teaching, the Departmental Science Advisors to the Ministry of Business Innovation and Employment—the major source of government funds for science—commented:

> Research that builds on what schools, families and whānau and students have contributed, including the cultural expressions of whānau and Pasifika households, will be important. More broadly, the threats to our physical and economic health and other dimensions of our social and cultural wellbeing should not be ignored. Not the least because the strength of our educational and social sectors underpins our recovery, there is a strong case for increased RSI in, for example, improved educational practices, social cohesiveness and the health of our cultural institutions. Such investment, of course, provides a natural vehicle for genuine research partnership with Māori. (Evans et al., 2021, pp. 6–7)

If this is the case, then we could do well to increase the investment in high quality, solutions-focused research, evaluation, and research and development. Often educational science is caught on the horns of a dilemma which reduces access to the funding. It can be seen as too applied for the basic science funding, yet educational sciences should be focused on solutions. Some of the distinctions usually made when identifying critical research do not adequately describe contemporary educational research and some areas of social science more broadly. For example, knowledge generation and applied research do not need to be mutually exclusive. New experimental designs and methods of what has been called Design-Based Research focus on solving pressing problems of practice in context, as well as generating new knowledge (Lai et al., 2020).

The four big problems for educational science to solve in our equity and excellence objectives identified in this last chapter are best solved using this complementary focus. Some solutions for the challenges and effective innovation are present in the system, but not consistently applied at scale. Such big problems require co-ordination of different methodologies and research and development sequences between many layers of the system. They are not easily placed into categorisations of "critical research", yet they are critical.

Our educational sciences could yet be another strength in the system. At the very least they could better contribute to bolstering and extending the strengths I have argued for here.

The claim made in this book is that we have strengths and we should build on them. It is a claim that the evidence for how we could solve our excellence and equity challenges means capitalising on these strengths. Becoming a higher quality highly equitable education system requires this for Aotearoa New Zealand.

References

Abrami, P. C., Bernard, R. M., Borokhovski, E., Waddington, D. I., Wade, C. A., & Persson, T. (2015). Strategies for teaching students to think critically: A meta-analysis. *Review of Educational Research*, 85(2), 275-314. https://doi.org/10.3102/0034654314551063.

Alton-Lee, A. (2003). Quality teaching for diverse students in schooling: *Best Evidence Synthesis Iteration (BES)*. Ministry of Education. https://www.educationcounts.govt.nz/publications/series/2515/5959

Auguste, B., Kihn, P., & Miller, M. (2010). *Closing the talent gap: Attracting and retaining top third graduates to careers in teaching. An international and market research-based perspective.* McKinsey & Company.

Belich, J. (writer, presenter). (1998). *The New Zealand Wars* [television]. NZ on Screen. https://www.nzonscreen.com/title/the-new-zealand-wars-1998/series

Benton, R. (1973). *Te tirohanga i te kōrerotanga o te reo rangatira i roto i ngā kainga Maori me ngā rohe | Survey of language use in Māori households and communities 1973-1978.* Te wāhanga kaupapa Māori | NZCER. https://www.nzcer.org.nz/benton

Berryman, M., Bidois, P., & Furlong, M. (1995). Tatari Tautoko Tauawhi: A Maori language reading tutoring programme. *Set: Research Information for Teachers,* (1), 1-6. https://doi.org/10.18296/set.0937

Bishop, R., Berrymen, M., Cavanagh, T., & Teddy, L. (2009). *Te Kotahitanga: addressing educational disparities facing Maori students in New Zealand. Teaching and Teacher Education. 25,* 734-742.

Borman, G. D., Gamoran, A., & Bowdon, J. (2008). A randomized trial of teacher development in elementary science: First-year achievement effects. *Journal of Research on Educational Effectiveness,* 1(4), 237-264.

Bronfenbrenner, U. (2009). *The ecology of human development: Experiments by nature and design.* Harvard University Press.

Bryant, J., Heitz, C., Sanghvi, S., & Wagle, D. (2020). *How artificial intelligence will impact K-12 teachers.* McKinsey and Co.

Bryk, A. S., Gomez, L. M., Grunow, A., & LeMahieu. P. G. (2015). *Learning to improve: How America's schools can get better at getting better.* Harvard Education Press.

Chamberlain, M. (2019). *PIRLS 2016: Reading literacy and the classroom. Ministry of Education.* https://www.educationcounts.govt.nz/__data/assets/pdf_file/0012/195888/Classroom-and-Practice_for-ECounts_UDb.pdf

Clay, M. (2007, Fall). International perspectives on the Reading Recovery program. *Journal of Reading Recovery,* 16–34. https://readingrecovery.org/wp-content/uploads/2016/12/JRR_7.1-Clay.pdf

Clements, K., Cooper, G., Corballis, M., Elliffe, D., Nola, R., Rata, E., & Werry, J. (2021, 31 July). *In defence of science. Listener,* 4.

Compton-Lilly, C. F., Mitra, A., Guay, M., & Spence, L. K. (2020). A confluence of complexity: Intersections among reading theory, neuroscience, and observations of young readers. *Reading Research Quarterly, 55*(S1), S185–S195. https://www.jstor.org/stable/48587614

Cooke, H. (2021, February 3). *Government releases the New Zealand histories that will be compulsory in schools from 2022.* Stuff. https://www.stuff.co.nz/national/politics/300220613/government-releases-the-new-zealand-histories-that-will-be-compulsory-in-schools-from-2022

Darling-Hammond, L. (2013). Developing and sustaining a high-quality teacher force. Prepared for the Global Cities Education Network. *Asia Society.* https://asiasociety.org/files/gcen-darlinghammond.pdf

Darling-Hammond, L., & Bransford, J. (2005). *Preparing teachers for a changing world: What teachers should learn and be able to do.* Jossey-Bass.

Darling-Hammond, L., Flook, L., Cook-Harvey, C., Barron, B., & Osher, D. (2020). Implications for educational practice of the science of learning and development. *Applied Developmental Science, 24*(2), 97–140. https://doi.org/10.1080/10888691.2018.1537791

Davison, M. (2021). *Teaching and learning history.* Ministry for Culture and Heritage. https://nzhistory.govt.nz/brain-food/teaching-and-learning-history,

Denny, S., Howie, H., Grant, S., Galbreath, R., Utter, J., Fleming, T., & Clark, T. (2018). Characteristics of school-based health services associated with students' mental health. *Journal of Health Services Research & Policy, 23*(1) 7–14. https://doi.org/10.1177/1355819617716196

Dowden, A. (2022). *Provision of internet connectivity and devices to learners: Evaluation report: A 2020 Covid-19 response.* Ministry of Education. https://www.educationcounts.govt.nz/publications/schooling2/digital-technology/evaluation-of-provision-of-connectivity-and-devices-a-covid-19-response

Dunlop, M. (2021, 28 July). *University academics' claim mātauranga Māori 'not science' sparks controversy.* Radio New Zealand. https://www.rnz.co.nz/news/te-manu-korihi/447898/university-academics-claim-matauranga-maori-not-science-sparks-controversy

Education Council. (2017). *Our code our standards: Code of professional responsibility and standards for the teaching profession.* https://teachingcouncil.nz/assets/Files/Code-and-Standards/Our-Code-Our-Standards-Nga-Tikanga-Matatika-Nga-Paerewa.pdf

Education Gazette. (2014). Ready to Read turns 50. *Education Gazette, 93*(3). https://gazette.education.govt.nz/articles/1H9ctj-ready-to-read-turns-50/#jumpto-a-brief-history

Education Review Office | Te Ihuwaka Education Evaluation Centre. (2021). *Learning in a Covid-19 world: Supporting secondary students as they return to the classroom.* Education Review Office. https://ero.govt.nz/our-research/learning-in-a-covid-19-world-supporting-secondary-school-students-as-they-return-to-the-classroom

Elley, W. B. (1992). *How in the world do students read? IEA study of reading literacy.* International Association for the Evaluation of Educational Achievement.

Ellis, G., & Bloch, C. (2021). *Neuroscience and literacy: An integrative view.* Transactions of the Royal Society of South Africa.

Enari, D., & Matapo, J. (2020). The digital vā: Pasifika education innovation during the COVID-19 pandemic. *MAI Journal, 9*(4). https://doi.org/10.20507/MAIJournal.2020.9.4.2

Engel, M., Claessens, A., Watts, T., & Farkas, G. (2016). Mathematics content coverage and student learning in kindergarten. *Educational Researcher, 45*(5), 293–300. https://doi.org/10.3102/0013189X16656841

Evans, G., Murdoch, R., & Spencer, H. (2021). *A resilient research, science & innovation sector enabling post-pandemic economic transformation.* Ministry of Business, Innovation & Employment. https://www.mbie.govt.nz/dmsdocument/11628-a-resilient-research-science-and-innovation-sector-enabilng-post-pandemic-economic-transformation

Fastnedge, D. (2020, July 8). *Small budgets, big ideas—what a viral porn awareness campaign tells us about New Zealand advertising.* The Conversation. https://theconversation.com/small-budgets-big-ideas-what-a-viral-porn-awareness-campaign-tells-us-about-new-zealand-advertising-141529

Fraillon, J., Ainley, J., Shulz, W., Friedman, T., & Duckworth, D. (2018). *Preparing for life in a digital world: IEA International Computer and Information Literacy Study 2018 International Report.* International Association for the Evaluation of Educational Achievement.

Freshwater, D. (2021, 26 July). *Vice-Chancellor comments.* University of Auckland. https://www.auckland.ac.nz/en/news/2021/07/26/vice-chancellor-comments.html

Fullan, M., Rincon-Gallardo, S., & Hargreaves, A. (2015). *Professional capital as accountability. Education Policy Analysis Archives, 23*(15). https://doi.org/10.14507/epaa.v23.1998

Gerrard, J. (2018). *Every 4 minutes: A discussion paper on preventing family violence in New Zealand.* Office of the Prime Minister's Chief Science Advisor.

Gerritsen, J. (2021, 5 July). *Hiring more Māori researchers 'needs its own dedicated funding'.* Radio New Zealand. https://www.rnz.co.nz/news/national/446190/hiring-more-maori-researchers-needs-its-own-dedicated-funding

Gluckman, P. (2017). *Towards a whole of government/whole of nation approach to mental health.* Office of the Prime Minister's Chief Science Advisor. https://cpb-ap-se2.wpmucdn.com/blogs.auckland.ac.nz/dist/f/688/files/2020/02/17-08-14-Mental-health-long.pdf

Glynn. T, (2021). *Living the Treaty: Personal reflections.* The New Zealand Psychological Society with Te Rū Rangahau.

Gould, S. J. (1989). *Wonderful life: The Burgess Shale and the nature of history.* W. W. Norton.

Haidt, J., & Paresky, P. (2019, January 10). *By mollycoddling our children, we're fuelling mental illness in teenagers.* The Guardian. https://www.theguardian.com/commentisfree/2019/jan/10/by-mollycoddling-our-children-were-fuelling-mental-illness-in-teenagers

Hattan, C., Alexander, P. A., & Lupo, S. M. (2024). Leveraging what students know to make sense of texts: What the research says about prior knowledge activation. *Review of Educational Research, 94*(1), 73–111. https://doi.org/10.3102/00346543221148478

Hattie, J. (2009). *Visible learning: A synthesis of over 800 meta-analyses relating to achievement.* Routledge.

Hattie, J. (2015). The applicability of visible learning to higher education. *Scholarship of Teaching and Learning in Psychology, 1*(1), 79–91. http://dx.doi.org/10.1037/stl0000021

Hennessy, S., & London, L. (2013). *Learning from international experiences with interactive whiteboards. The role of professional development in integrating the technology.* OECD Education Working Papers, No. 89. OECD Publishing. http://dx.doi.org/10.1787/5k49chbsnmls-en

Hood, N. & Hume, R. (2024). *The illusion of inclusion: The experiences of neurodivergent children and those supporting them in Aotearoa New Zealand's education system.* The Education Hub. https://theeducationhub.org.nz/wp-content/uploads/2024/05/Ed-Hub_Illusion-of-Inclusion-report_v2_low-res.pdf

Horn, S., & Veermans, K. (2019). Critical thinking efficacy and transfer skills defend against 'fake news' at an international school in Finland. *Journal of Research in International Education, 18*(1), 23–41. https://doi.org/10.1177/1475240919830003

Hunia, R., Salim, S., McNaughton, S., Menzies, R., Gluckman, P., & Bardsley, A. (2020). *Addressing Rangatahi education: Challenges after COVID-19. A partnership report by Ngāti Whātua Ōrākei and Koi Tū: The Centre for Informed Futures.* University of Auckland. https://informedfutures.org/wp-content/uploads/pdf/Addressing-rangatahi-education.pdf

Jang-Jones, A. & McGregor, A. (2019). *PISA2018: New Zealand Students' Wellbeing—School climate & student mindsets of 15-year-olds.* Ministry of Education. https://www.educationcounts.govt.nz/__data/assets/pdf_file/0005/196628/PISA-2018-NZ-Students-Wellbeing.pdf

Jesson, R., McNaughton, S., Rosedale, N., Zhu, T., & Cockle, V. (2018b). A mixed-methods study to identify effective practices in the teaching of writing in a digital learning environment in low income schools. *Computers and Education, 119* (April), 14–30. https://doi.org/10.1016/j.compedu.2017.12.005

Jesson, R., McNaughton, S., Wilson, A., Zhu, T., & Cockle, V. (2018a). Improving achievement using digital pedagogy: Impact of a research practice partnership in New Zealand. *Journal of Research on Technology in Education, 50*(3), 183–199. http://doi.org/10.1080/15391523.2018.1436012

Jones, A. (2020). *This Pākehā life: An unsettled memoir.* Bridget Williams Books.

Jones, A., & Jenkins, K. (2011). *He kōrero: Words between us: First Māori–Pākehā conversations on paper.* Huia Publishers.

Jones, A., & Middleton, S. (eds.). (2009). *The kiss and the ghost: Sylvia Ashton-Warner and New Zealand.* NZCER Press.

Kirkham, S., with May, S. (2015). *PISA 2015: The science context for PISA.* Ministry of Education. https://www.educationcounts.govt.nz/__data/assets/pdf_file/0017/180611/PISA-2015-Science-Context_v2.pdf

Kukutai, T., McIntosh, T., Boulton, A., Durie, M., Foster, M., Hutchings, J., Mark-Shadbolt, M., Moewaka Barnes, H., Moko-Mead, T., Paine, S-J., Pitama, S., & Ruru, J. (2021). *Te Pūtahitanga: A Tiriti-led science policy approach for Aotearoa New Zealand.* Ngā Pae o te Māramatanga. https://www.maramatanga.ac.nz/sites/default/files/CB_TePutahitanga_A4_2021_inner_Digital_final.pdf

Lai, M. K., McNaughton, S., Jesson, R., & Wilson, A. (2020). *Research-practice partnerships for school improvement: The Learning Schools Model.* Emerald Publishing.

Lee, C. (2007). *Culture, literacy, and learning: Taking bloom in the midst of the whirlwind.* Teachers College Press.

Lipson, B. (2020). *New Zealand's education delusion. How bad ideas ruined a once world-leading school system.* New Zealand Initiative. https://www.nzinitiative.org.nz/reports-and-media/reports/new-zealands-education-delusion-how-bad-ideas-ruined-a-once-world-leading-school-system

Little, H. (2020). *Promoting children's risky play in outdoor learning environments.* The Education Hub. https://theeducationhub.org.nz/promoting-childrens-risky-play-in-outdoor-learning-environments/

McCormick, E. H. (1959). *New Zealand literature: A survey.* Oxford University Press.

McDonald, G. (2002). Dr C E Beeby and the quality of education. *Set: Research Information for Teachers,* (2), 25–27. https://doi.org/10.18296/set.0715

MacDonald, M. (2016). *Elwyn Richardson and the early world of creative education in New Zealand.* NZCER Press.

McGregor, A., & Webber, A. (2019). *What do we know about discrimination in schools?* Ministry of Education. https://www.educationcounts.govt.nz/publications/series/he-whakaaro/he-whakaaro-what-do-we-know-about-discrimination-in-schools

McGrew, S., Ortega, T., Breakstone, J., & Wineburg, S. (2017). The challenge that's bigger than fake news. Civic reasoning in a social reasoning environment. *American Educator*, Fall, 4–9.

McNaughton, S. (2011). *Designing better schools for culturally and linguistically diverse children: A science of performance model for research*. Routledge.

McNaughton, S. (2018). *Instructional risk in education. Why instruction can fail*. Routledge.

McNaughton, S. (2020). *The literacy landscape in Aotearoa New Zealand: What we know, what needs fixing and what we should prioritise*. Office of the Prime Minister's Chief Science Advisor Kaitohutohu Mātanga Pūtaiao Matua kit e Pirimia. https://cpb-ap-se2.wpmucdn.com/blogs.auckland.ac.nz/dist/f/688/files/2020/01/The-Literacy-Landscape-in-Aotearoa-New-Zealand-Full-report-final.pdf

McNaughton, S. (2022). What we can do to realise our excellence and equity goals in literacy. pp.62-77. *New Zealand Annual Review of Education* / Te Arotake-ā-tau o Te Ao o te Mātauranga i Aotearoa. https://doi.org/10.26686/nzaroe.v28.8278

McNaughton, S. & Li, J. (2018). Well-being in schools: Chinese and New Zealand approaches. *Educational Research for Policy and Practice, 21*, 125–141. https://doi.org/10.1007/s10671-021-09296-8

McNaughton, S., Parr, J., Timperley, H., & Robinson, V. (1992). Beginning reading and sending books home to read: A case for some fine tuning. *Educational Psychology, 12*(3 & 4), 239–247.

McNaughton, S., Zhu, T., Rosedale, N., Oldehaver, J., Jesson, R., & Greenleaf, C. (2019). Critical perspective taking: Promoting and assessing online written argumentation for dialogic focus. *Studia Paedagogica (special issue: Better Learning through Argumentation), 24*(4). 119–141. https://doi.org/10.5817/SP2019-4-6

Mair, D., Smillie, L., La Placa, G., Schwendinger, F., Raykovska, M., Pasztor, Z., & Van Bavel, R. (2019). *Understanding our political nature*. Publications Office of the European Union. http://doi.org/10.2760/374191

Manning, M., Wong, G. T. W., Fleming, C. M., & Garvis, S. (2019). Is teacher qualification associated with the quality of the early childhood education and care environment? A meta-analytic review. *Review of Educational Research*, 89(3), 370–415. http://dx.doi.org/10.3102/0034654319837540

Manning, R. F., & Cooper, G. W. (2018, 19 Oct). *Submission to the Māori Affairs Select Committee: The teaching of 'New Zealand colonial histories' and more broadly, Māori histories in New Zealand school curricula (particularly at secondary school level)*. New Zealand Parliament Māori Affairs Select Committee Inquiry into the Teaching of New Zealand Colonial Histories.

May, S. (2017). *PISA2015: Collaborative problem solving report*. Ministry of Education. https://www.educationcounts.govt.nz/__data/assets/pdf_file/0009/183483/PISA-Collaborative-Problem-Solving-Report.pdf

May, S. (2019). *PISA2018: New Zealand Summary Report—System Performance & Equity*. Ministry of Education. https://www.educationcounts.govt.nz/__data/assets/pdf_file/0006/196629/PISA-2018-NZ-Summary-Report.pdf

Meissel K., Bergquist, M., Kumarich, J., et al. (2021). *The Growing Up in New Zealand COVID-19 Wellbeing Survey: Part 2: Education*. Growing Up in New Zealand. https://assets.website-files.com/63a70013e473f3b2807218ee/63cfc48f189af13de413a155_GUINZ_Wellbeing_Survey_Part2_FINAL NOV 2_2.pdf

Ministry of Business, Innovation & Employment. (2018). *Research, science and innovation system performance report 2018*. https://www.mbie.govt.nz/dmsdocument/1499-research-science-and-innovation-system-performance-report-2018

Ministry of Education. (n.d.). *Aotearoa New Zealand's histories and Te Takanga o Te Wā*. https://www.education.govt.nz/our-work/changes-in-education/aotearoa-new-zealands-histories-and-te-takanga-o-te-wa/

Ministry of Education (2007). *The New Zealand curriculum*. Learning Media. http://nzcurriculum.tki.org.nz/The-New-Zealand-Curriculum

Ministry of Education. (2017a). *Te whāriki: He whāriki mātauranga mō ngā mokopuna o Aotearoa—Early childhood curriculum*. https://assets.education.govt.nz/public/Documents/Early-Childhood/Te-Whariki-Early-Childhood-Curriculum-ENG-Web.pdf

Ministry of Education. (2017b). *Update of Te Whāriki: Report on the engagement process*. https://assets.education.govt.nz/public/Documents/Early-Childhood/ONLINE-Te-Whariki-Update-Long-v21A.PDF

Ministry of Education. (2018). *2018 Teaching and Learning International Survey: New Zealand Year 7-10 teacher wellbeing*. https://www.educationcounts.govt.nz/__data/assets/pdf_file/0014/200156/NZ-Year-7-10-Teacher-Wellbeing_TALIS-2018-Focus-Report.pdf

Ministry of Education. (2019a). *He whakaaro: Education insights. How environmentally aware are New Zealand students?* https://www.educationcounts.govt.nz/__data/assets/pdf_file/0010/193564/He-Whakaaro-How-environmentally-aware-are-New-Zealand-students.pdf

Ministry of Education. (2019b). *Equity index technical report*. https://www.educationcounts.govt.nz/__data/assets/pdf_file/0003/196005/Equity-Index-Technical-Report-Final.pdf

Ministry of Education. (2020a). *He whakaaro: Education insights. What do we know about bullying behaviours in New Zealand?* https://www.educationcounts.govt.nz/publications/series/he-whakaaro/he-whakaaro-what-do-we-know-about-bullying-behaviours-in-new-zealand

Ministry of Education. (2020b). *TIMSS 2018/19: Mathematics Year 5*. https://www.educationcounts.govt.nz/publications/schooling2/large-scale-international-assessments/timss-201819-mathematics-year-5

Ministry of Education. (2020c). *He whakaaro: Education insights. The importance of identity, language and culture for ākonga Māori.* https://www.educationcounts.govt.nz/__data/assets/pdf_file/0003/198642/He-Whakaaro-Importance-of-Maori-identity-language-and-culture-for-akonga-Maori.pdf

Ministry of Education. (2021a). *He whakaaro: Education insights. Student learning during COVID-19: Literacy and maths in Years 4–10.* https://www.educationcounts.govt.nz/__data/assets/pdf_file/0004/208147/He-Whakaaro-Student-learning-during-COVID-19-Literacy-and-maths-in-Years-4-10.pdf

Ministry of Education. (2021b). *Groundbreaking kawenata signed with Ngā Iwi.* https://www.education.govt.nz/news/groundbreaking-kawenata-signed-with-nga-iwi/

Ministry of Education. (2022). *What is the value of y? Year 9 students' strengths and weaknesses on mathematics questions.* https://www.educationcounts.govt.nz/__data/assets/pdf_file/0016/213181/What-is-the-value-of-y-Year-9-students-strengths-and-weaknesses-on-mathematics-questions.pdf

Ministry of Education. (2023a). *A short synthesis of findings from our large education studies.* https://www.educationcounts.govt.nz/publications/schooling2/large-scale-international-assessments/a-short-synthesis-of-findings-from-our-large-education-studies

Ministry of Education. (2023b). *Reading literacy at Year 5: New Zealand's participation in PIRLS 2021.* https://www.educationcounts.govt.nz/__data/assets/pdf_file/0015/221037/PIRLS-2021-Reading-literacy-Year-5.pdf

Mhuru, M. (2019). *He whakaaro education insights: The importance of identity, language and culture for ākonga Māori.* Ministry of Education. https://www.educationcounts.govt.nz/publications/series/he-whakaaro/he-whakaaro-the-importance-of-identity-language-and-culture-for-akonga-maori

Mourshed, M., Chijioke, C., & Barber, M. (2010). *How the world's most improved school systems keep getting better.* McKinsey & Company. https://www.mckinsey.com/industries/education/our-insights/how-the-worlds-most-improved-school-systems-keep-getting-better

Mutch, C. (2004). The Rise and Rise of Early Childhood Education in New Zealand. *Citizenship, Social and Economics Education, 6*(1), 1–11. https://doi.org/10.2304/csee.2004.6.1.1

O'Brien. G. (2007). *A nest of singing birds: 100 years of the New Zealand School Journal.* Learning Media.

O'Connor, P., Anderson, M., Freebody, K., & Ginns, P. (2020). *Replanting creativity in post normal times.* Unpublished research report. The Centre for Arts and Social Transformation, University of Auckland.

OECD, (2018). "What makes high-performing school systems different", in *World class: How to build a 21st-century school system.* OECD Publishing. https://doi.org/10.1787/9789264300002-3-en.

OECD, (2019). *TALIS 2018 Results (Volume I): Teachers and school leaders as lifelong learners.* TALIS, OECD Publishing. https://dx.doi.org/10.1787/1d0bc92a-en.

OECD, (2020). *Trustworthy AI in health. Background paper for the G20 AI Dialogue.* Digital Economy Task Force. https://www.oecd.org/health/trustworthy-artificial-intelligence-in-health.pdf

OECD. (2022). *Teachers' salaries.* http://dx.doi.org/10.1787/f689fb91-en

Olson, D. R. (2003). *Psychological theory and educational reform: How school remakes mind and society.* Cambridge University Press.

Pearce, R., & Miles, F. (2015). 7-year retrospective review of quad bike injuries admitted to Starship Children's Hospital. *The New Zealand Medical Journal (Online), 128* (1414), 44-50. https://pubmed.ncbi.nlm.nih.gov/26117390/

Pihama, L., Cameron, N., & Te Nana, R. (2019). *Historical trauma and whānau violence.* Issues Paper 15. New Zealand Family Violence Clearinghouse, University of Auckland.

Puzio, K., Colby, G. T., & Algeo-Nichols, D. (2020). Differentiated literacy instruction: Boondoggle or best practice? *Review of Educational Research, I*(4), 459–498. https://doi.org/10.3102/0034654320933536

Read, L. (2006). New Zealand film: National identity and the films of Vincent Ward: The development of New Zealand's national cinema attests to the changing nature of New Zealand's national identity. *Metro Magazine*, 148, spring, 124+.

Redding, C. (2019). A teacher like me: A review of the effect of student–teacher racial/ethnic matching on teacher perceptions of students and student academic and behavioral outcome. *Review of Educational Research, 89*(4), 499–535. http://doi.org/10.3102/0034654319853545

Rei, T., & Hamon, C. (1993). In Women together: A history of women's organisations in New Zealand. *Nga ropu wahine o te motu / edited by Anne Else Wellington, N.Z. : Historical Branch, Dept. of Internal Affairs and Daphne Brasell Associates Press*, 1993. https://nzhistory.govt.nz/women-together

Reimers, F. M., & Schleicher, A. (2020). *Schooling disrupted, schooling rethought: How the Covid-19 pandemic is changing education.* OECD. https://education4resilience.iiep.unesco.org/resources/2021/schooling-disrupted-schooling-rethought-how-covid-19-pandemic-changing-education

Rendall, S., Medina, E., Sutcliffe, R., & Marshall, N. (2020). *Mathematics | Year 5: Trends over 24 years in TIMMS. Findings from TIMMS 2018/19.* Ministry of Education. https://www.educationcounts.govt.nz/__data/assets/pdf_file/0003/205707/TIMSS-2018-Year-5-Mathsc.pdf

Reznitskaya, A., Kuo, L. J., Clark, A. M., Miller, B., Jadallah, M., Anderson, R. C., & Nguyen-Jahiel, K. (2009). Collaborative reasoning: A dialogic approach to group discussions. *Cambridge Journal of Education, 39*(1), 29–48.

Robinson, M. V. J., McNaughton, S., & Timperley, H. (2011). Building capacity in a self managing system: The New Zealand experience. *Journal of Educational Administration, 49*(6), 720-738.

Robinson, V., Hohepa, M., & Lloyd, C. (2009). *School leadership and student outcomes: Identifying what works and why. Best Evidence Synthesis Iteration [BES]*. Ministry of Education. www.educationcounts.govt.nz/__data/assets/pdf_file/0015/60180/BES-Leadership-Web-updated-foreword-2015.pdf

The Royal Society Te Apārangi Expert Advisory Panel. (2021). *Pāngarau mathematics and tauanga statistics in Aotearoa New Zealand. Advice of refreshing the English-medium Mathematics and Statistics learning area of the New Zealand Curriculum.* https://www.royalsociety.org.nz/assets/Pangarau-Mathematics-and-Tauanga-Statistics-in-Aotearoa-New-Zealand-Digital.pdf

Sachdeva, S. (2021, 17 November). *Royal Society investigation into mātauranga Māori letter sparks academic debate.* Newsroom. https://newsroom.co.nz/2021/11/17/royal-society-investigation-into-matauranga-maori-letter-sparks-academic-debate/

Salmond, A. (2018). *Two worlds: First meetings between Māori and Europeans,* 1642-1772. Viking.

Schleicher, A. (2018), Teachers' well-being, confidence and efficacy. In *Valuing our teachers and raising their status: How communities can help.* OECD Publishing. https://www.oecd.org/education/valuing-our-teachers-and-raising-their-status-9789264292697-en.htm

Schleicher, A. (2018b). *World class: How to build a 21st-century school system*, Strong Performers and Successful Reformers in Education series. OECD Publishing. https://www.oecd.org/education/world-class-9789264300002-en.htm

Schmidt, W. H., Nathan A. Burroughs, N. A., Zoido, P., & Houang, R. T. (2015). The role of schooling in perpetuating educational inequality: An international perspective. *Educational Researcher, 44*(7), 371–386. http://doi.org/10.3102/0013189X15603982

Shelton, R.C., Cooper, B. R., Stirman, S. W. (2018). The sustainability of evidence-based interventions and practices in public health and health care. *Annual Review of Public Health, 39*, 55-76. https://doi.org/10.1146/annurev-publhealth-040617-014731

Sheridan, S. M., Smith, T. E., Moorman Kim, E., Beretvas, S. N., & Park, S. (2019). A meta-analysis of family-school interventions and children's social-emotional functioning: Moderators and components of efficacy. *Review of Educational Research,* 89(2), 296-332. http:// doi.org/10.3102/0034654318825437

Simon, J., & Smith, L. T. (Eds.). (2001). *A civilising mission? Perceptions and representations of the New Zealand Native Schools system.* Auckland University Press.

Simpson, M.M. (1962). S*uggestions for teaching reading in infant classrooms.* Department of Education.

Sims, S. (2021). *Lowering teacher stress through CPD & teamwork.* Teacher Development Trust. https://tdtrust.org/2021/04/09/lowering-teacher-stress-through-cpd-teamwork/

Speare-Cole, R. (2020, June 13). *Alumni of top London private schools call on bosses to 'teach about white privilege' and 'decolonise the canon'.* The Standard. https://www.standard.co.uk/news/uk/racism-private-schools-london-alumni-letters-a4466276.html

Speigelhalter, D. (2019). *The art of statistics: Learning from data.* Penguin Random House/Pelican Books.

Thomas, S., Meissel, K., & McNaughton, S. (2019). *He whakaaro education insights: What affects how often mothers read books to their pre-schoolers?* Ministry of Education. https://www.educationcounts.govt.nz/__data/assets/pdf_file/0008/196757/He-Whakaaro-What-affects-how-often-mothers-read-books-to-their-pre-schoolers.pdf

Tomorrow's Schools Independent Taskforce. (2018). *Our schooling futures: Stronger together Whiria Ngā Kura Tūātinitini.* Ministry of Education. https://conversation.education.govt.nz/assets/TSR/Tomorrows-Schools-Review-Report-13Dec2018.PDF

Universities New Zealand & NZQA. (2022). *The impact on first-year university performance of changes to the UE standard in response to Covid-19.* https://www.universitiesnz.ac.nz/sites/default/files/uni-nz/The%20impact%20of%20changes%20to%20the%20UE%20standard.pdf

Verschaffel, L., Schukajlow, S., Star, J. Van Dooren, W. (2020). Word problems in mathematics education: A survey. *ZDM Mathematics Education, 52,* 1–16. https://www.semanticscholar.org/paper/Word-problems-in-mathematics-education%3A-a-survey-Verschaffel-Schukajlow/d64eef56e6217c6b87a1d7b9377251ac93b165b3

Vygotsky, L. S. (1978). *Mind in society.* Harvard University Press.

Walker, C. G., Fletcher, B. D, Cha, J. E., Waldie, K. E., Morton, S. M. B., Peterson, E. R., Bullen, P., Prickett, K., Meissel, K., Fenaughty, J., Paine, S. J. (2023). G*rowing Up in New Zealand. Now we are 12: Experiences of the COVID-19 pandemic and young people's wellbeing. Snapshot 6.* https://www.growingup.co.nz/growing-up-report/experiences-of-the-covid-19-pandemic-and-young-peoples-wellbeing

Walker, R. (2008). *Paki Harrison: Tohunga whakairo: The story of a master carver.* Penguin Group.

Warren, G. *Early 19th century Māori literacy.* Auckland War Memorial Museum - Tāmaki Paenga Hira. https://www.aucklandmuseum.com/discover/collections/topics/early-19th-century-maori-literacy

Webber, A. (2021). *He Whakaaro: Student learning during COVID-19: Literacy and maths in Years 4-10 .* Ministry of Education. https://www.educationcounts.govt.nz/publications/series/he-whakaaro/he-whakaaro-student-learning-during-covid-19

Wenmoth, D. (2021). *Systemness: Achieving a sustainable digital ecolearning system for New Zealand*. Future Makers.

White, T. (2017, February 17). *School Journals not always as appreciated as they are now*. Stuff. https://www.stuff.co.nz/national/education/89463359/school-journals-not-always-as-appreciated-as-they-are-now

Wilson, W., Madjar, I., & McNaughton, S. (2016): Opportunity to learn about disciplinary literacy in senior secondary English classrooms in New Zealand, *The Curriculum Journal, 27*(2), 204–228. https://doi.org/10.1080/09585176.2015.1134339

Wylie, C. (2012). *Vital connections: Why we need more than self-managing schools*. NZCER Press.

Wynn, K. (2016, February 27). *Bringing risk back into children's lives*. The New Zealand Herald. https://www.nzherald.co.nz/nz/bringing-risk-back-into-childrens-lives/MGZBCDLRVCBZLZBBNVSVJAPQ7I/

Wyse, D. & Bradbury, A, (2022). Reading wars or reading reconciliation? A critical examination of robust research evidence, curriculum policy and teachers' practices for teaching phonics and reading. *Review of Education, 10*(1). http://doi.org/10.1002/rev3.3314

Index

Aboriginal and Torres Strait Islander schools 38–39
accelerated progress 40
adaptive expertise 90–91
adaptiveness 21
advertisements for social messaging 71–72
"affordances" 67, 73
agency of children 24, 29, 72, 73, 80
AI-powered tools 97, 112–14
ako 42, 43
ākonga Māori 59, 69, 114
    achievement 1, 28, 29, 46, 56–57, 84–85
    cultural identity 6, 38, 39, 47, 103
    educational success 39, 40, 54, 87
    engagement 2, 28, 85
    in English classrooms 108
    in schooling system largely created by non-Māori 6, 38, 39
    Waipapa Taumata Rau University of Auckland 43, 61
    see also Te Kotahitanga
Ashton-Warner, Sylvia 21, 22, 25, 27

Beeby, Clarence 24, 35, 70–71
Belich, James, New Zealand Wars documentary 11
belonging at school 1, 28, 47, 91
Benton, Richard 44–45
Best Evidence Synthesis programme 43–44
best practice 81
Better Public Service 40
bias 3, 56, 82
biculturalism
    evaluation of the strength of trying to be bicultural 84–87
    indicators 39
    in mainstream English-medium classrooms 42–44, 46, 47

Te Whāriki 71
tokenism 39, 48
trying to be bicultural 6, 38–52, 69, 103, 115, 116
variability in being bicultural 111
bilingual commitment 39
Bishop, Russell 28–30
"Black Lives Matter' protests 47
Boards of Trustees
    development as a form of creativity 71
    differential access to knowledge and funding 58, 94
    role and responsibilities 15, 17, 54, 57, 87
bonding, human 24
Bronfenbrenner, Uri 55, 58, 88
bullying 1, 76, 91, 106, 113

capability building 3, 30, 50, 92, 93, 96, 97, 99, 103, 105, 108
    readily available levers 97, 110–12
    teaching 94–96
challenges to being better 92–96
"child-centred" 24–25, 69, 76, 97, 105, 106–08, 116
    arguments against a child-centred approach 76, 77, 78
    Beeby's remodelled education system 35, 70–71
    child-centred books 25–26
    child-centred new-entrant practice 31–32
    COVID-19 educational practice 32–35
    Elwyn Richardson's child-centred teaching 27–28
    origins of child-centredness in Aotearoa New Zealand 35–37
    threats to being child-centred 79

children
- development 110
- experiences 6
- identity 6
- see also learning from only some children

citizenship 13, 41
Clarke, George 50
Clarke, John 65
collaboration
- collaborative reasoning 97, 101, 106–08
- collaborative skills 55–57
- collaborative strength in schools 56, 61–62, 102–03
- relationships and collaboration between schools 57–59, 89, 102–03
- between researchers and policymakers 6, 59–61

Collective Teacher Efficacy (CTE) 103
collectivism 27, 57, 62, 85, 101
- Gaelic practices 62
- Māori 61, 62, 74

colonial schooling 5, 20, 21, 26, 51, 69; see also Native Schools
colonisation 40, 74
- colonial elements of collectivism and co-operation 62
- colonial negative influences on valuing children 36–37
- impacts on Māori 37, 39, 40, 84, 86, 105

Communities of Learning | Kāhui Ako 19, 58–59
community–school relationships 6, 9, 57–58, 59, 85, 87, 88, 116
connections 63
content knowledge 10, 14, 47, 49, 76, 77, 78, 79, 80–81, 112
- Pedagogical Content Knowledge (PCK) 91, 99

contexts 2–3, 9
- local contexts 2–3, 9, 10, 12, 20, 21, 47, 81, 82, 83, 93, 104–05, 116
- shifting between contexts 41

continuous improvement 3, 53, 68, 96, 99, 111
corporal punishment 36

COVID-19 pandemic 7, 47, 61, 106
- child-centred educational response 32–35, 72
- creative responses 71–74, 90
- delivery of resources to tamariki, families, and whānau 83, 89, 114–15
- impact on attractiveness of teaching 98
- importance of partnerships 89
- lockdowns 4, 20, 32, 61, 97, 114–15, 117
- measures of achievement before and after lockdowns 33, 115
- NCEA impacts 34–35, 114
- see also online teaching and learning

creativity 6–7, 21, 27–28
- Digital Learning Objects (DLOs) 66–67, 72
- in the educational system 65–66, 70–71
- evaluating the strength 90–92
- in gifted and talented students 64
- having a go 64–65
- in Manaiakalani schools 67–69, 72
- national creativity 69–71
- School Journals 68, 69–70
- sustained and at scale 68–69
- see also innovation

cross-age tutoring 42
cultural capital 88
cultural worlds 41
culturally-embedded knowledge 81–82
curiosity 24
curriculum 8, 9, 23, 85
- curriculum design 9–10, 11–12, 13, 73, 90, 91, 97, 99, 104, 116
- curriculum "refresh" 2, 8, 12, 49, 83, 86, 104–05
- local curriculum 9, 10–12, 73, 80
- variable interpretations 111
- see also New Zealand Curriculum (Ministry of Education, 2007)

data 28, 29, 30, 31, 32, 38–39, 81, 110
- ākonga Māori 47, 56–57, 84–85
- on collaborative problem solving 56–57, 62

equity 56–57
Learning Schools Model 53–54
Pasifika students 56–57
timely and fit-for-purpose data 83, 111
wellbeing data 91, 115
see also OECD
decoding 14, 25
design-based interventions 53
Design-Based Research 117
digital divides
unequal access to infrastructure, connectivity and devices 32–33, 74
usage patterns by students from less privileged communities 33
digital pedagogies 2, 106, 112, 113
Digital Learning Objects (DLOs) 66–67, 72
disabilities 1–2, 92
discrimination 47, 62, 84
diversity 24

early childhood education 2, 3, 26, 71, 109–10
interactive reading 88
for Māori 40
risky play 36
see also Kōhanga Reo; Te Whāriki
Education Act 1989 44
Education and Workforce Select Committee (2019) 12
Education Portfolio Work Programme 87
Education Review Office 15
educational success 56, 76
equitable distributions 54
judging success 53–54
Māori 39, 40, 54, 84–85
Pasifika 54
Elley, Warwick 31–32
emotional development of students 23, 36, 37, 79, 82, 88, 95, 101, 113–14
empathy 101, 113
employment pathways 40
engagement 3, 14
hapū and iwi 58
English curriculum 70

English-medium schools 45, 46
enabling ākonga Māori achievement 42, 43, 44, 85, 103
equity 24, 67–68, 70, 79, 80, 88, 96, 117, 118
access to and use of digital media 114
ākonga Māori 56–57, 84–85, 104
child-centred teaching 76–77, 79, 80
equitable distributions of success 54
excellence and equity goals 2, 6, 17, 25, 30, 75–76, 90, 93, 96, 98, 108, 109–10, 111, 117, 118
literacy 14–15, 28, 108–09
local curriculum 105
low equity profile 1–2, 4–5, 18, 28, 76, 93
Māori-medium education 46
Pasifika students 56–57, 104
relationships and collaboration 56–57, 58, 61–62, 88
trying to be bicultural 51–52, 84, 85
variability 93, 96, 105
equity index 94
ethnic inequalities 18, 19, 56
examinations
Proficiency Exam 70
senior secondary examinations 2, 84, 86
see also National Certificates of Educational Achievement (NCEA)
excellence 13, 18, 28, 40, 56, 86, 93; *see also under* equity

families
engaging in children's early reading 18, 28, 54–55, 88
intercultural relationships 51–52
partnerships 6
teacher relationships 54, 73, 89
see also whānau
farm accidents 36
Finland 2, 3, 99, 106–07, 108
Forest Lake School Te Kura o Roto Ngahere 41
Fred Dagg 64–65
funding of schools 2, 5

gender inequalities 18, 108
    gender gap in new-entrant practice 31
gender stereotyping 37
Gerrard, Dame Juliet 61
gifted and talented students 64
Gluckman, Sir Peter 60–61
Glynn, Ted 51–52
Grace, Patricia 47, 70
    Butterflies 81–82
Growing Up in New Zealand study 88

Harrison, Pakariki (Paki) 20–21
high school *see* secondary education
history 10
    Aotearoa New Zealand histories 10–13, 49, 70, 83, 86, 101, 104–05
    Tudor England 11
Hohi game 11–12
Holsted, Iona 110–11
honesty 24
Hughes, Peter 16
    Free and Frank Advice and Policy Stewardship 16
human rights 24

identity
    Māori cultural identity 6, 38, 39, 47, 84
    students 6, 14, 15, 24–25
Ihimaera, Witi 47, 70
implementation science 96
improvement science 96
independence 24
individualism 62
information literacy 4
initial teacher education 94, 95, 101
innovation 6–7, 24, 26, 27, 29, 71, 74, 85, 90, 103, 116, 117, 118
    digital pedagogies 2, 67, 68–69, 72, 73, 113
    literacy instruction 13, 17, 18, 27
    Native Schools 21–22, 26, 41, 42, 44
    online learning 72, 73
    scalability 26, 27, 69, 118
    see also creativity
inquiry pedagogy 77–78, 100, 105

inquiry plus guided teaching 77
integrity 24
interactive whiteboards 34, 73
International Association for the Evaluation of Educational Achievement (IEA) 17–18, 31
Irish settlers, collectivist Gaelic practices 62

Jones, Alison 52

Ka Hikitia—Ka Hāpaitia, the Māori Education Strategy 83
Kāhui Ako | Communities of Learning 19, 58–59
kapa haka 46–47, 64, 86
kawanatanga 51
Kawenata between Ministry of Education and Ngā Iwi 83
key competencies 95, 101
    relating to others key competency 16, 43
    wellbeing key competencies 16–17, 43
kindergarten 71, 107
kindness 24
kōhanga reo 45
kura kaupapa Māori 40, 45, 84
    achievement of ākonga 46

language experience approach to writing 27
learning from only *some* children 23–37
    evaluation of the strength of learning from children 76–80
    see also "child-centred"
Learning Schools Model (LSM) 53
Lemon, Ruth, Hohi game 11–12
life-course approach to change 97, 102, 108–10
literacy 1, 4, 56
    effect of student background on achievement 28
    Māori 35, 50, 74
    whānau and family engagement 18, 28, 54–55

literacy instruction
    child-centred books 25–27
    Common Practice Model 104
    critical literacy 97, 101, 106–08
    differentiated instruction in early phonics teaching 77, 79
    Effective Literacy Practices in Years 1–4 66
    Elwyn Richardson's child-centred, integrated teaching 27–28
    high quality but low equity outcomes 18, 28
    international comparisons of effectiveness 17–18
    mirror texts and window texts 13–15, 21, 47, 82, 105
    provisions for being local 82
    Reading Recovery early intervention 60, 68
    see also reading; writing
living conditions 32, 84
local strengths
    Aotearoa New Zealand history teaching 10–13
    curriculum 9, 10–12, 73, 80
    evaluation of the strength of being local 80–84
    expertise 6, 8, 96
    increasing clarity and detail of being local 104–05
    learning from local conditions 59
    local control of schools 15, 19, 57–58
    local knowledge and experiences of students 10, 14, 47, 49, 76, 77, 78, 79, 80–81, 112
    mirror texts and window texts 13–15, 21, 47, 82, 105
    reasons why being local is a strength 20–22
    School Journals 69–70
    taking an idea beyond the local 69
    variable and inconsistent quality in being local 12, 93
    see also schools – self-managing (locally controlled) schools

mahi hononga (connection work) 61
"man alone" narrative 36–37, 62, 74
mana motuhake 83
Manaiakalani schools 67–69, 72
Māori
    achievement gaps 1, 5, 40
    collectivism 61, 62, 74
    colonisation impacts 36, 39, 40, 84, 86, 105
    creativity 64, 74
    cross-agency strategy for success 87
    educational designs 6
    intergenerational trauma 36
    Ka Hikitia—Ka Hāpaitia, the Māori Education Strategy 83
    research partnership 117
    writers 47
    see also ākonga Māori; Kōhanga Reo; Kura Kaupapa Māori; Te Kotahitanga; te reo Māori; Wānanga
Māori Language Act 1987 40
Māori-medium education 40, 85, 86, 97, 103–04
    definition 48
mātauranga Māori 49–50, 86, 87, 103
material hardship 1, 2, 5, 62, 67–68, 102, 116; *see also* poverty
mathematics 3, 8, 67
    achievement 68, 76, 81, 100, 110–11
    achievement before and after lockdowns 33, 115
    Common Practice Model 104
    high quality instruction but low equity outcomes 18, 19
    inquiry and discovery learning 77
    literacy 56
    low progress in the primary years 19
    negative number concept 9
    teaching 95–96, 100
    word problems 82
Matthew effects 58, 109–10
Maui 62, 74
meaning-making 53, 103, 111–12
Measures of Effective Teaching (MET) project 29

media literacy 4
"mesosystem" 55, 58
metacognition 77-78
microsystems 57, 58
Ministry of Education 16, 27, 30, 34, 43, 45, 60, 71, 74, 114, 115
  partnerships with iwi 83-84, 86-87
mirror texts 13-15, 21, 47, 82
ML-powered tools 97, 112-14
multiculturalism 41

National Certificates of Educational Achievement (NCEA)
  COVID-19 impacts 34-35, 114
  Level 2 40, 84, 94, 108
  standards 48
Native Schools 5, 11, 21-22, 25, 41-44, 51, 61
  legacy in bicultural practices 41, 42, 43, 44
neurodivergent students 2, 101
new entrants 31-32
New Zealand Curriculum (Ministry of Education, 2007) 47
  science curriculum 49-50
  see also key competencies
New Zealand Initiative (NZI) 76, 77, 78, 80
New Zealand School Journals 10
New Zealand Warriors example of negative number 9
New Zealand Wars documentary (Belich) 11
Ngā-Kura-ā-Iwi 45
Ngāti Whātua Ōrākei 114
norms 23, 107
  cultural norms 40
"number 8 wire" 65
numeracy 1

OECD 1, 2, 4, 24, 28, 56, 73, 76, 78, 85, 89, 91, 99, 108, 115, 116
Olson, David 24, 78
online teaching and learning
  communities of practice 107
  developed by teachers 20, 73
  feedback from students 33-34, 72
  local content 20, 73
  moving from online to face to face 92
  personalised online engagement 34
  research 117
  "rewindable" resources 34, 72
  role of families and whānau 89
  see also COVID-19
ōritetanga 51

partnerships 6, 53-54, 84
  collaborative problem solving 55-57
  hearing reading at home 54-55
  learning from local conditions 59
  Manaiakalani schools 68
  Ministry of Education and iwi 83-84, 86-87
  relationships and collaboration between schools 57-59
  Te Tiriti o Waitangi 51, 52
  see also relationships
Pasifika students 60, 114, 115
  achievement gaps 1, 5, 56-57
  educational success 54
  in English classrooms 108
  Waipapa Taumata Rau University of Auckland 43, 61
Pasifika writers 48
Pause, Prompt, and Praise 54-55
Pedagogical Content Knowledge (PCK) 91, 99
peer tutoring 42, 43, 55
  duality 43-44
Performance-Based Research Fund (PBRF) 86, 87, 116
performance science 96
perseverance 24
personal development of students 23
perspective-taking 101, 107
phonics teaching 77, 79
policymakers, collaboration with researchers 6, 59-61
Pompallier, Bishop 50
pornography online, child safety ads 27, 71-72
poverty 5, 32, 62, 109; see also material hardship

primary education 2, 3, 110
    generalist and specialist teaching 95–96, 100
    low mathematics achievement 19, 100
problem solving
    collaborative problem solving 55–57, 62
    computer game-based format 4
    local cycles 18
professional development and learning 8, 89, 9
Programme for International Student Assessment (PISA) 1, 55–56, 108
Puketapu, Karen 44

quad-bike accidents 36

racism 3, 52, 62, 70
reading 4, 101
    achievement 68, 76, 108–09
    achievement before and after lockdowns 33, 115
    child-centred books 25–27, 65–66
    comprehension 10, 14, 17, 82
    decoding 14, 25
    hearing reading at home 54–55, 88
    indicators of biculturalism 47–48
    international comparisons 56
    mirror texts and window texts 13–15, 21
    phonics teaching 77, 79
    Te Rauparaha 74
    text content and reader's background knowledge 14, 47
    whānau and family engagement in early reading 18, 28, 54–55, 88
    see also literacy instruction
Reading Recovery early intervention 60, 68
Reading Together programme 55
Ready to Read series 25–27, 41
relationships 23, 24
    evaluating the strength 87–89
    relating to others key competency 16, 43

    relationships and collaboration between schools 57–59
    school–community relationships 6, 9, 57–58, 59, 85, 87, 88
    teacher relationships with whānau and families 6, 9, 54
    tuakana-teina relationships 41, 42–43, 44, 46, 61
    see also partnerships; whanaungatanga ren 24
research
    educational research needs and funding 116–18
    Māori research 86, 87
    Performance-Based Research Fund (PBRF) 86, 87, 116
    researchers' collaboration with policymakers 6, 59–61
    by teachers 99–100
Research, Science, and Innovation (RSI) 116, 117
resources 8, 19, 20, 21, 26, 27, 38, 65
    digital resources 20, 34, 68, 72, 73, 74, 83, 96
    in Māori-medium education 46
    variability in distribution 46, 56, 58, 62, 92, 93–94, 96, 104, 109
respect 8, 24, 29, 39, 41, 59, 84, 85
Richardson, Elwyn 27–28, 66
risky play 36

Salmond, Anne 35
scalability 30, 38, 81, 92, 93, 96, 105
    community "ownership" of schools 19
    creativity 68–69
    digital pedagogy 1, 67
    innovation 26, 27, 69, 118
    teaching quality 95
School Journals 10, 68, 69–70
    writers and artist contributors 69–70
schools
    community relationships 6, 9, 57–58, 59, 85, 87, 88, 116
    competitiveness between schools 19, 58, 89
    groups of schools 6, 9, 15, 19

local hubs to pool teaching and learning resources 19
low-decile schools 53, 67–69, 72, 94, 108
relationships and collaboration between schools 57–59, 89, 102–03
self-managing (locally controlled) schools 15, 19, 57–58, 59, 87, 96, 102, 103
see also Boards of Trustees; kura kaupapa Māori
science 3
    achievement 76, 100
    curriculum 8, 49–50, 87
    evaluating and designing scientific enquiry 56
    inquiry and discovery learning 77, 78
    learning from children 78
    literacy 56
    teaching 95, 100
    variability in being local 82
science advisors 60–61, 102, 117
    Chief Science Advisor to the Prime Minister 61
Scottish settlers
    collectivist Gaelic practices 62
    influences on child-centredness 35
seatbelts for children in back seat of vehicles 36
secondary education
    abolition of Proficiency Exam 70
    high school leaving level 40
    leaving qualification 71
    teaching 96, 100–01
self-regulation 2, 44, 101, 107, 113
Simon, Judith 21–22, 43
Simpson, Myrtle, *Suggestions for Teaching Reading in Infant Classes* (1963) 26–27
Smith, Linda Tuhiwai 21–22, 43
social development of students 23, 79, 82, 88, 95, 101, 107, 113, 114
social impact advertisements 27
social media 27, 106
socialisation 23, 24, 36, 37, 88
socioeconomic status (SES) 18, 19, 54, 56, 57, 62, 68, 72, 93, 104, 108, 114

Spiegelhalter, David 18, 80–81
statistics education 18, 80–81
Statistics learning area 8
stereotypes 82
stewardship role of government agencies 16–17
strengths 4–7
students
    agency 24, 29, 72, 73, 80
    diverse students 44
    effects of background 28, 32, 56–57, 62
    gifted and talented students 64
    local knowledge and experiences 10
    new entrants 31–32
    see also ākonga Māori; Pasifika students
success *see* educational success
Suggestions for Teaching Reading in Infant Classes (Simpson, 1963) 26–27
sustainability 58, 92, 93, 96, 105, 113
    creativity 68–69

taha Māori 39, 47, 48
Tāne-nui-ā-Rangi wharenui, Waipapa Taumata Rau University of Auckland 20–21
tāngata Tiriti 39, 41
Tatari, Tautoko, Tauawhi 54–55
Te Hurihanginui 30
Te Kete Ipurangi 43
Te Kotahitanga 28–30, 85
Te Kura Kaupapa Māori o Hoani Waititi 45
Te Mataaho-a-Iwi 83
Te Rauparaha 74
te reo Māori 21, 39, 40, 44–46, 51, 84, 103
    Benton Report 44–45
    learning in te reo 48
    official language of Aotearoa New Zealand 40
    suppression in schools 40, 42, 51
    use by teachers 86
    see also kōhanga reo; kura kaupapa Māori
Te Rūnanga Nui o Ngā Kura Kaupapa Māori 45, 84

Te Tiriti o Waitangi | Treaty of Waitangi 39, 50–51, 52, 62, 84, 105
  articles 51
Te Wānanga o Aotearoa 45
Te Wānanga o Raukawa 45
Te Whare Wānanga o Awanuiārangi 45
Te Whāriki 71, 109
teachers
  accountability 112
  adaptive expertise 90–91
  codes of conduct 17
  collaboration 57–59, 61–62, 102–03
  curriculum design skills 9–10, 11–12, 13, 73, 90, 91, 97, 99, 104, 116
  knowledge of te reo and tikanga Māori 86
  Māori teachers 85, 97, 101–02, 103–04
  Native School teachers 21–22
  online resource development during COVID-19 lockdowns 20, 73
  Pasifika teachers 97, 101–02, 103–04
  pay 98–99, 112
  practising certificates 86, 111
  selection and qualifications 98–99
  teacher relationships with whānau and families 6, 9, 54, 73, 89
teaching
  creative teaching 90–91
  didactic teaching 34, 73, 77
  differentiating instruction for individual learners 76–77, 79, 80, 85, 112
  embedded or apprenticeship style 20–21
  giving more control to the learner 76
  inquiry plus guided teaching 77
  local contexts 9, 10, 12, 20, 21, 47, 81, 82, 83, 93, 104–05, 116
  national expectations for teaching local history 12–13
  raising the status of teaching 97–103
  research and evidence orientation 99–100
  specialist teaching 100–01
  supported pathways 101–02
  variability in quality 93, 94–96

Teaching and Learning Research Initiative (TLI) 116
tertiary education 34, 40, 43, 45, 73, 86, 101
tikanga Māori 86
tino rangatiratanga 51
tokenism 39, 48
Tomorrow's Schools policy 57–58, 89, 103
Treaty of Waitangi see Te Tiriti o Waitangi | Treaty of Waitangi
tuakana-teina relationships 41, 42–43, 44, 46, 61
  duality 43–44

UNESCO Mahatma Gandhi Institute of Education for Peace and Development 113–14
Universities New Zealand 87
University Entrance 84, 86

values 23, 41
  cultural values 40
variability 4–5, 30, 91–96, 105, 108, 109
  achievement 93–94
  collaboration between schools 58–59
  high-quality practices in schools 97
  quality of teaching 93, 94–96
  readily available levers to reduce variability 97, 110–12
  resources 93–94
  variable and inconsistent quality in being local 12, 82, 93
violence to children 36
Vygotsky, Lev 43

Waipapa Taumata Rau The University of Auckland 20–21, 87, 111
  tuakana programme 43, 61
Waitangi Tribunal 51, 84
Wānanga 45
wellbeing of students 1, 85, 90, 91, 111, 113, 114, 115
  differing concepts 23–24
  implementation at system level 16–17
  preparedness for NCEA exams after lockdowns 34–35, 114

Wendt, Albert 48
whaikōrero (speechmaking) 61
whānau 103
    engaging in children's early reading 18, 28, 54–55, 88
    intercultural relationships 51–52
    partnerships 6
    teacher relationships 6, 9, 54, 73, 89
    see also families
whanaungatanga 24; *see also* relationships
Wilson, Aaron 13–14
window texts 13–15, 21, 82, 105
writing
    achievement 67, 68
    achievement measures before and after lockdowns 33, 115
    Digital Learning Objects (DLOs) 66–67
    language experience approach 27
    phonics teaching 77, 79

Zone of Proximal Development 43

www.ingramcontent.com/pod-product-compliance
Lightning Source LLC
Chambersburg PA
CBHW080636230426
43663CB00016B/2890